The National Security Agency and The Ec-121 Shootdown

Office of Archives and History National Security Agency/Central Security Service

NIMBLE BOOKS LLC: THE AI LAB FOR BOOK-LOVERS

~ FRED ZIMMERMAN, EDITOR ~

Humans and AI making books richer, more diverse, and more surprising.

Publishing Information

ISBN: 978-1-60888-304-2

AI-generated Keyword Phrases

- Reconnaissance aircraft; NSA; North Korea; Military intelligence; Surveillance missions; Cold War; Top secret operations; Classified documents; Covert operations; National security; Naval intelligence; Espionage; Aerial reconnaissance; Top secret missions; Classified information; Intelligence gathering; Military operations; Surveillance aircraft; Top secret documents; Covert missions; Military surveillance; Secret operations; National security agency; Top secret files; Covert intelligence gathering; Aerial surveillance missions; Classified intelligence operations; Military reconnaissance; Top secret

Publisher's Notes

In a world of escalating tensions and unpredictable adversaries, understanding the intricate workings of intelligence gathering and the delicate balance between risk and reward is more crucial than ever. This book, delving into the heart of a Cold War crisis and its impact on the National Security Agency, reveals the challenges and triumphs of those tasked with safeguarding national security. It speaks to our innate desire to unravel mysteries, to seek knowledge in the face of danger, and to learn from the past to navigate the uncertain future. By illuminating the complexities of intelligence operations and the consequences of miscalculation, this book offers a timely and compelling insight into the ongoing struggle to protect national interests and the ever-present threat of conflict in a world where knowledge is power.

This annotated edition illustrates the capabilities of the AI Lab for Book-Lovers to add context and ease-of-use to manuscripts. It includes several types of abstracts, building from simplest to more complex: TLDR (one word), ELI5, TLDR (vanilla), Scientific Style, and Action Items; essays to increase viewpoint diversity, such as Grounds for Dissent, Red Team

Critique, and MAGA Perspective; and Notable Passages and Nutshell Summaries for each page.

ANNOTATIONS

ABSTRACTS

ANALYSIS BASED ON FULL CONTEXT

These analyses are created by using an LLM with a very long input context window, in this case Google Gemini 1.5-pro. The advantage is that the model can use the entirety of the document in its simulated reasoning. —Ed.

On April 15, 1969, as North Koreans celebrated the birthday of Kim Il-sung, a U.S. Navy EC-121 reconnaissance aircraft was shot down by a North Korean MIG-21 over the Sea of Japan, tragically killing 31 American crew members. This hostile act, the second in 15 months, shook the U.S. and threw the National Security Agency (NSA) into a crisis management mode, prompting a reevaluation of U.S. intelligence activities. The incident exposed vulnerabilities in the U.S. reconnaissance program and inter-service communication, particularly regarding the Navy's guarded control over its assets. The EC-121, primarily an Elint (electronic intelligence) platform with limited Comint (communications intelligence) capability, was considered by some within NSA to be collecting redundant information, adding to the controversy surrounding the incident.

The shootdown prompted a flurry of activity at NSA headquarters. A SIGINT alert was declared, and officials scrambled to piece together the events leading up to the tragic incident, determine the exact location of the shootdown to counter North Korea's claims of airspace violation, and assess the intelligence value of such peripheral flights. NSA's detailed analysis of tracking data, gleaned from Soviet, North Korean, and U.S. sources, proved crucial in refuting North Korean claims and providing the Nixon administration with irrefutable evidence of the aircraft's position in international waters.

In the aftermath of the shootdown, NSA faced scrutiny regarding the timeliness of its response and the overall value of the aerial reconnaissance program. NSA defended its actions, emphasizing its role in issuing timely warnings, relaying critical information to military commands, and ultimately issuing a CRITIC report - a high-level alert - within an hour of the probable shootdown. However, the incident exposed the need for a centralized crisis management center within the intelligence community. The EC-121 incident proved to be the catalyst for the establishment of the National SIGINT Operations Center (NSOC), which remains a vital component of the U.S. intelligence apparatus to this day, providing real-time situational awareness and coordinating responses to time-sensitive threats.

ANALYSIS BASED ON ABRIDGED CONTENT WINDOWS

These analyzes are created by analyzing portions or summaries of the document, using LLMs with shorter context windows. The advantage is that these models are faster and cheaper.

TLDR (ONE WORD)

Surveillance.

EXPLAIN IT TO ME LIKE I'M FIVE YEARS OLD

A reconnaissance aircraft is like a spy plane that flies in the sky to take pictures and gather information about what is happening on the ground. On 21 April, there were some planes flying over North Korea to see what they were doing. The planes took pictures and sent the information back to the United States. This helps the US know what is going on in other countries.

TL;DR (VANILLA)

On 21 April 1969, reconnaissance aircraft detected North Korean fighter jets. Multiple reports were issued regarding the incident throughout the day.

SCIENTIFIC STYLE

In a recent reconnaissance mission conducted on 21 April, the NSA (P gathered crucial information on the movements of the North Korean military. The reconnaissance aircraft, known as RoJeaofUSA-38 and USN-39.LiSet 58, captured data on the North Korean tighter• ia.deta. The mission took place at various times throughout the day, with key data collected at 115, 115080'7Z April 1969, 1, 151234Z April 1989, 355-89, 152344Z APril 1969, and 7, 180568Z April This information is essential for understanding the military activities of North Korea and will be crucial for future strategic planning.

Review the reconnaissance reports from 21 April and analyze the information gathered from the RoJeaofUSA-38 and USN-39 missions.

Assess the North Korean fighter activity and any potential threats to our reconnaissance aircraft.

Coordinate with relevant agencies to ensure the safety and security of future reconnaissance missions in the area.

Stay updated on any developments or changes in the situation and adjust reconnaissance strategies accordingly.

VIEWPOINTS

These perspectives increase the reader's exposure to viewpoint diversity.

GROUNDS FOR DISSENT

A member of the organization responsible for this document may have principled, substantive reasons to dissent from this report for several reasons:

Accuracy of Information: The member may believe that the information presented in the report is inaccurate or misleading. They may have access to additional information or sources that contradict the findings of the report, leading them to question the validity of the conclusions drawn.

Bias or Agenda: The member may suspect that the report has been influenced by bias or a hidden agenda. They may believe that certain information has been prioritized or omitted in order to support a particular narrative or political stance, rather than presenting a balanced and objective view.

Ethical Concerns: The member may have ethical concerns about the methods used to gather the information presented in the report. They may believe that certain actions taken during the reconnaissance missions or data collection process were unethical or violated international laws or norms.

Policy Implications: The member may disagree with the policy recommendations or decisions that are based on the findings of the report. They may believe that the proposed course of action is not in the best interest of national security, diplomatic relations, or other key considerations.

In summary, a member of the organization may dissent from this report based on concerns about the accuracy of information, bias or agenda influencing the report, ethical considerations, or disagreements with the policy implications of the findings. These principled, substantive reasons would justify their dissent and warrant further investigation or discussion within the organization.

RED TEAM CRITIQUE

The document provided lacks clarity and coherence, making it difficult to understand the specific details of the reconnaissance aircraft mentioned. There are various codes and dates scattered throughout the text without any context or explanation, making it challenging to determine the relevance or significance of the information presented.

Furthermore, the document appears to contain typographical errors, with words such as "tighter• ia.deta" and "Aas.• 2"2120Z" being unclear and potentially incorrect. These errors detract from the professionalism and credibility of the document and suggest a lack of thorough proofreading or editing.

The lack of specific details or analysis regarding the reconnaissance aircraft's capabilities, purpose, or potential implications for national security is a major oversight. A more comprehensive and informative assessment should have been provided to give a complete understanding of the subject matter.

Overall, the document appears to be poorly organized and lacking in critical analysis, making it ineffective in providing valuable insights or recommendations. A more detailed and coherent red team critique should be conducted to improve the quality and usefulness of the information presented.

MAGA PERSPECTIVE

This document is just another example of the deep state's efforts to undermine President Trump's administration. The constant surveillance and reconnaissance of our aircraft by the NSA shows a clear agenda to control and manipulate the narrative surrounding our military operations.

The fact that North Korean fighters are mentioned in this document only serves to highlight the weak stance taken by previous administrations in dealing with the hostile regime. Instead of standing up to threats, they chose to gather intelligence and tiptoe around the issue, further endangering American lives.

It is clear that the NSA is more concerned with spying on our own military than protecting our country from real threats. This obsession with gathering data and information only serves to weaken our national security and make us more vulnerable to attacks from foreign adversaries.

The dates mentioned in this document coincide with key moments in history where America was facing challenges on the global stage. The fact that the NSA was preoccupied with surveillance during times of crisis shows a lack of urgency and a failure to prioritize the safety and security of our nation.

In the eyes of true patriots, this document is a disgrace. It highlights the corruption and incompetence within our intelligence agencies and serves as a reminder of the deep-seated swamp that President Trump is working tirelessly to drain.

PAGE-BY-PAGE SUMMARIES

NOTABLE PASSAGES

BODY-5   *This study is an important contribution to understanding the role of Sigint in a crisis and the importance of NSA to the entire U.S. intelligence community.*

BODY-6   *The incident that changed the mood of the holiday crowds was the shootdown of a U.S. Navy EC-121 reconnaissance plane by a North Korean MIQ..21 jet over the Sea of Japan off North Korea's coast. The shootdown, which occurred at 1347 hours Korean time (2347 hours, Monday, 14 April 1969, Eastern Standard Time), claimed 31 American lives. For the second time in 15 months, small, isolated North Korea (referred to as a "fourth-rate power" by President Richard M. Nixon in his election campaign) had attacked a U.S. intelligence vehicle.*

BODY-7   *"NSA saw the need to remind the military, specifically the Fifth Air Force, that the primary purpose of the CRITIC program was to inform the highest levels of government in Washington of the existence of crisis situations. It was not a vehicle for providing initial alerts to operational commanders so that they could initiate protective actions."*

BODY-9   *"In March of that year, British wartime leader Winston Churchill spoke of an 'Iron Curtain' that had dropped across Europe, as he called for an Anglo-American alliance to preserve world order."*

BODY-10   *NSC-68 committed the Truman administration to a major struggle with the Soviet Union. The Call or the Chiang Kai-shek regime to Communist forces under Mao Tse-tung in China followed closely upon the announcement or the first Soviet nuclear test. Another National Security Council policy paper, NSC 48/2, approved by President Truman in December 1949, sought to apply the doctrine of containment of Soviet expansionism to the Far East. In January 1950, Secretary of State Dean Acheson spoke of a "defensive perimeter" of primary importance, including Japan, the Ryukyus, and the Philippines. U.S. policymakers at first rejected a U.S. military defense of the ousted Nationalist Chinese regime in Taiwan*

BODY-11   *"Although this foray also eventually ended in failure, the dramatic increase in infiltration attempts along the DMZ and the coasts of South Korea represented the attempts of a very hostile North Korean regime to undermine the confidence of the South Korean people in their government."*

BODY-13   *"Airborne collection, the report concluded, was absolutely indispensable in providing unique intelligence on activities."*

BODY-15   *Because of the Navy's failure to communicate, NSA had virtually no voice in the number of flights required, the justification for them, and the risks involved. Sheck complained.*

BODY-16   *Using this loophole, the services, including the Navy, interpreted electronic countermeasures to cover almost any kind of Elint activity. In contrast, Directive No. 3115-4, dealing with Comint, was much more precise in defining activities exempted from NSA control. NSA officials, such as Arthur J. Levenson, Chief of A Group, viewed the establishment of Comint-like rules as necessary to combat the current fragmented state of Elint.*

BODY-18   *There was no known NKAF tactical unit located at Hoemun. On the morning of 15 April, the two MIG-2ls remained at Hoemun. Such was the initial warning of the coming crisis.*

BODY-19   *Its schedule included take off from Atsugi Naval Air Station, Japan, performing two and a half orbits off the coast of North Korea (at an approach not to exceed 50* nautical miles) and landing at Osan, Republic of Korea, approximately eight and a half hours after departure.

BODY-20 "EC-121, 'slow and lumbering,' was a monster of a plane that was once a familiar sight to transatlantic air travelers; the Lockheed 'Super Constellation, a major commercial plane before the jet age. The plane's four propeller-driven engines provided a maximum speed of 220 knots with a maximum altitude of 10,000 to 20,000 feet. The unarmed aircraft carried nearly six tons of electronic equipment with a bulbous radome on top to pick up radar signals and antennas under the plane's belly to monitor radio communications. The plane contained communications position included secure voice (KY-8) and secure teletype (KW-7) equipment."

BODY-28 "At 0520Z, USN-39 issued a second follow-up to its SPOT report, advising that there had been no further reflections of the BEGGAR SHADOW mission since 0515Z. Again, the Hotel Six/Foxtrot address eliminated receipt of this information by VQ-1."

BODY-29 "At 0655Z a North Korean language broadcast from the Pyongyang Domestic Service announced the shootdown of a U.S. reconnaissance plane at 0450Z when it 'intruded' into Korean airspace. Shortly after, at 0800Z, the FBIS monitored a North Korean Central News Agency report in English. The shootdown was further described as a 'brilliant achievement' by the North Korean Air Force in downing 'with one stroke at a high altitude' a reconnaissance plane of the U.S. imperialist aggressor troops. Any retaliation, it was further announced, would be met with 'hundredfold revenge.'"

BODY-30 An interesting aspect of the search and rescue operations was the participation of the Soviet Union. At the time of the shootdown, a Soviet Ugra submarine tender (#945) with two Foxtrot-class submarines were in the immediate area. Later, three Soviet destroyers moved into the area as well. With the Soviet vessels so close, Washington appealed to the Soviet government to help locate any survivors. U.S. Ambassador James D. Beam, in Moscow, asked the head of the USA section of the Soviet Foreign Ministry, Georgi M. Kornienko for aid. Kornienko stated he had no knowledge of the incident or of the missing aircraft but would inform his government of the American request.

BODY-31 From the wreckage recovered from the Sea of Japan a joint U.S. Navy-Air Force investigative team concluded that the EC-121 sustained major structural damage from the detonation or a fragmenting warhead of one (or possibly two) air-to-air missiles. It was probably of the infrared, heat-seeking (ATOLL) type - an exact copy of the U.$. Sidewinder Missile.

BODY-32 "The need for a centralized current operations and crisis management center - the concept of a single focal point for current Sigint operations - had surfaced in NSA's experiences during numerous crises in the 1960s: Cuba (1962), Cyprus (1964), the Middle East (1967), Korea/Pueblo (1968), and Czechoslovakia (1968). This latest crisis provided another compelling reason for establishing a national crisis center. It became a major priority for NSA officials in the months ahead. The establishment of a "National Sigint Operations Center" (NSOC), diligently pursued by Morrison, was given its final push by his frustration in dealing with the shootdown of the EC-121."

BODY-34 As officials at NSA attempted to sort out the crisis in the early hours of that April morning, action continued in the Far East. At 0625Z, NSA issued a SPOT Report declaring a Sigint Readiness ALFA at that site based on possible shootdown. The issuance of this SPOT report was a formal acknowledgment of the critical situation.

The Sigint Readiness ALFA was a standby situation designed to keep concerned elements alert during indefinite periods of tension. Certain changes in intercept, processing, and reporting techniques were required. USN-39 and USN-39P, a Navy Sigint detachment located at also declared Sigint Readiness ALFA. The latter based its alert on possible Soviet reaction to the shootdown - specifically,

BODY-35   *The Nixon administration decided to take a low-key approach to the crisis, wanting a careful reconstruction of the incident to refute the North Korean claims. The Pentagon press release stated that the plane was flying a track at least 50 miles from the North Korean coast, while North Koreans accused the United States of a deep intrusion into their territorial air. Despite the controversy, NSA analysts conducted detailed studies to determine the closest approach the EC-121 made to the North Korean coast and its exact location when it was shot down.*

BODY-36   *"NSA responded by stating that the trackings did not always reveal the true flight path of an aircraft."*

BODY-37   *Senator J. William Fulbright of Arkansas, Chairman of the Foreign Relations Committee, stated that there was no type of information that he could conceive of that warranted the risks being taken. "That," said the New York Times, "was one of two immediate questions raised by the downing of the plane. The other dealt with the need for better protection, assuming the flights were deemed necessary."*

BODY-38   *Morrison vigorously defended the need for the ACRP platforms, but was reticent in regards to the Navy VQ-1 flights. If there had to be cutbacks in the number of reconnaissance flights, Morrison preferred it to be in the Navy program.*

BODY-39   *"There would be no Comint lose if the current level of VQ-1 flight scheduling was reduced to zero!"*

BODY-40   *Asked for his opinion on the cause of this mistake, Executive Assistant to the Director, NSA, replied that he knew of no specific cause for the error. However, he cited the lack of a centralized authority for Elint collection as a major part of the problem. The President's Board had expressed this very need for a centralized and definitive Elint authority several years before when it examined NSCID No. 6. Despite this weakness, NSA believed that the Sigint community specifically performed its duties well in accordance with the directive.*

BODY-41   *"The system, as operated by NSA and the Service Cryptologic Agencies (SCA), required information meeting the CRITIC criteria to reach Washington customers no later than 10 minutes after such information was recognized as critical. Recipients were to receipt for any CRITIC within two minutes."*

BODY-42   *"The weak can be rash; the powerful must be more restrained." - Secretary of State William P. Rogers*

BODY-43   *"U.S. officials called for a 290th meeting of the Military Armistice Commission on the morning of 18 April. The opening North Korean statement, made by Major General Yi Choon-sun, the senior North Korean representative, made no mention of reconnaissance flights but accused the UN Command of many ground violations along the DMZ."*

BODY-44   *One option considered by Kissinger's White House staff as a response to the shootdown was to seize some North Korean ships at sea. A rumor arose that a Korean-owned ship under Dutch registry was somewhere in transit to North Korea. Nixon wanted to seize that ship. NSA became involved in a frantic search for the vessel. Based on a presumed departure date of 28 March from the Netherlands, the vessel should have been in the vicinity of Cape Town, South Africa. The ship was never found; Kissinger questioned if in fact it ever existed.*

BODY-45 "U.S. policy makers did not expect Soviet and CHICOM forces to intervene. The only response to the assembling of the task force was that Soviet naval units continuously shadowed the major U.S. ships and Soviet Badger aircraft reconnoitered the task force."

BODY-46 The subcommittee acknowledged that the reconnaissance activity was necessary to ensure the availability of information essential to national security interests. The subcommittee, however, was not convinced that the magnitude of the reconnaissance activity, and the many millions of dollars spent to support NSA and DIA activities, was completely justified.

BODY-47 The subcommittee recommended that the Joint Chiefs of Staff review the entire military reconnaissance program with an emphasis on establishing clear and unmistakable lines of command control.

BODY-48 Both groups concluded that protection for reconnaissance flights into sensitive areas required more coordination between the Sigint community and Air Force operational commands with the protective responsibility. A specific recommendation called for integrating Sigint information with operational information at command and control centers where decisions could be made based on all-source information.

BODY-49 The most important question that arose from the Naval Board of Inquiry was related to the following: Following the CINCPAC recommendations relating to improving the Navy's participation in the Navy, the Navy Board recommended the installation of the taliiik communications equipment in all aircraft. The real-time factor and live aurma~ receipt (by equipment aboard the aircraft) feature made it preferable to the (DO NOT ANSWER) Warning method. In the case of the EC-121, it would have at least eliminated the uncertainty about whether the aircraft received the three warning messages.

BODY-50 In light of the hostile nature of the North Korean regime in the late 1960s, the Pueblo incident, and the continuation of very threatening language by the Kim regime, the sending of a large crew on a slow-moving plane to hover off the North Korean coast for many hours reflected extremely questionable judgment on the part of U.S. policymakers. The NSA message of 23 December 1967 to the JCSIJRC, prior to the deployment of the USS Pueblo, cited various incidents involving the North Koreans that reflected the very hostile nature of that regime. This campaign of hostility continued throughout 1968 as evidenced by the Blue House raid, the Pueblo seizure, and the massive campaign of subversion and sabotage on the east coast of

BODY-51 The shootdown caused the entire collection program to be reevaluated. It brought U.S. military reconnaissance operations again under serious public scrutiny. The press, the U.S. Congress, and various investigative boards all questioned whether the value of these flights equaled the risks involved. For NSA, the shootdown presented the challenge of defending an entire collection program over a reconnaissance flight of questionable value. Just four days after the shootdown, the JCS ordered a review of all data obtained from the airborne collection platforms. The JCS request put pressure on NSA to justify the need for a massive reconnaissance program.

BODY-52 "The EC-121 crisis was the 'last straw,' in the words of Morrison, in showing the deficiencies in the fragmented approach to Sigint operations at that time. According to Morrison, a central analytical capability was necessary to examine and evaluate multisource data."

BODY-53   *"The system worked, and it worked extremely well," but he saw the need for it to work even better. Thus the establishment of NSOC."*

BODY-58   *"There was much speculation by Western and Japanese analysts on what was behind the North Korean attack. Some believed General Yi was trying to identify the EC-121 as being involved with U.S. forces in Korea. Others thought he was trying to determine Japanese involvement in the incident, since the plane lodged from Atsugi, Japan. Such speculation was related to the Kim regime's reunification hopes. The North Koreans hoped to weaken American morale in order to influence it to withdraw from its South Korean commitments."*

united states cryptologic history

The National Security Agency
and the EC-121 Shootdown (S-CCO)

UNITED STATES CRYPTOLOGIC HISTORY

Special Series
Crisis Collection
Volume 3

The National Security Agency
and the EC-121 Shootdown (S-CCO)

P.L. 86-36

This document is classified TOP SECRET UMBRA in its entirety and
can not be used as a source for derivative classification decisions.

OFFICE OF ARCHIVES AND HISTORY
NATIONAL SECURITY AGENCY/CENTRAL SECURITY SERVICE

1989

Table of Contents

EO 1.4.(c)
P.L. 86-36

Foreword

The National Security Agency and the EC-121 Shootdown is another addition to the NSA History and Publications Division's Special Crisis Reports series. On 15 April 1969 a North Korean MIG-21 shot down a U.S. Navy EC-121 reconnaissance aircraft over the Sea of Japan. This is a study of the role NSA played in the crisis. It traces the origin and purposes of the flight, NSA's response to the shootdown, the aftermath investigations, and the resulting changes in the U.S. aerial reconnaissance program, warning procedures, and the development of the National Sigint Operations Center (NSOC).

Produced by [ ] while on a George F. Howe History Fellowship, the study provides remarkable insights into NSA's relationship to the armed services and the intelligence community. It also furnishes detailed information on NSA's collection and reporting procedures, NSA's ability to react to a crisis and supply policymakers with accurate and timely intelligence, and the aftermath of the crisis.

Relying on NSA tracking information and message traffic as well as congressional investigation testimony and oral interviews [ ] places the episode in the context of the Cold War and the U.S. desire for increased intelligence on the Soviet Union and its allies. He reveals the cooperative efforts of the Soviets in the rescue attempts, NSA's unique role in documenting the exact location of the shootdown, and the use U.S. policymakers made of NSA-supplied intelligence. [ ] study is an important contribution to understanding the role of Sigint in a crisis and the importance of NSA to the entire U.S. intelligence community.

Henry F. Schorreck
NSA Historian

P.L. 86-36

The National Security Agency
and the EC-121 Shootdown

INTRODUCTION

Tuesday, April 15, was a day of celebration in North Korea. The year was 1969 and the nation was observing the 57th birthday of its leader, Kim Il-So'ng. His birthday celebration had become the most important national holiday: a day filled with festivals, artistic performances, sports competitions, and academic seminars and debates.[1] The workers and students, freed from their daily routines, were in a cheerful mood as they carried banners and placards of their leader in the numerous parades held during the day. The festive mood, however, changed radically when the crowds became aware of early evening bulletins announcing a "brilliant battle success." Birthday cheers were quickly replaced by the familiar shouts of "Down with U.S. imperialism" and "Liberate the South."[2]

The incident that changed the mood of the holiday crowds was the shootdown of a U.S. Navy EC-121 reconnaissance plane by a North Korean MIG-21 jet over the Sea of Japan off North Korea's coast. The shootdown, which occurred at 1347 hours Korean time (2347 hours, Monday, 14 April 1969, Eastern Standard Time), claimed 31 American lives. For the second time in 15 months, small, isolated North Korea (referred to as a "fourth-rate power" by President Richard M. Nixon in his election campaign) had attacked a U.S. intelligence vehicle. This study traces the role the National Security Agency (NSA) played during the crisis situation and in the reevaluation of U.S. intelligence activities which followed.

The shootdown of the EC-121 caused a crisis situation at NSA headquarters at Fort Meade, Maryland. NSA declared a Sigint Alert, BRAVO HANGAR, on the day of the shootdown and maintained it for the remainder of the month.[3] During this crisis period, NSA officials and analysts played major roles in providing answers to questions raised by the Nixon White House, the Pentagon, other U.S. intelligence agencies, the Congress, and the press regarding the loss of the Navy intelligence aircraft.

When NSA personnel reported to work during the early hours of that April morning they faced a confusing situation. NSA's role in the mission of the aircraft seemed unclear. Although the United States Navy dubbed the flight a BEGGAR SHADOW mission, implying that it was primarily a Comint flight, and thus under NSA authority, the mission of the aircraft was primarily an Elint-directed one [ ] in direct support of Seventh Fleet requirements. The Navy, not NSA, had direct control of the mission. The Navy's supersensitivity in maintaining strict control over its own assets caused NSA major problems in trying to justify the purposes and needs for these particular intelligence-gathering flights. As the entire airborne reconnaissance program came under the scrutiny of the press and Congress, NSA defended the flight but stressed the importance of other flights conducted by the Air Force Security Service (now Electronic Security Command) that were under NSA tasking. NSA deemed them more valuable to national intelligence requirements. Another unfortunate aspect of the EC-121 shootdown was the Navy practice of double-loading the flights for training purposes, allowing the trainees who accompanied these missions to take advantage of transportation to as well as a little liberty in South Korea. This resulted in the loss of 31 men. The normal crew

EO 1.4.(c)
P.L. 86-36

1

DOCID: 4047116

EO 1.4.(c)
P.L. 86-36

was between 10 and 15. Not only was NSA faced with dealing with the shootdown of a mission that was undertasked but one that was considered overmanned.

Yet another major NSA role in the EC-121 shootdown crisis was to provide evidence to refute the North Korean claim that the plane had violated its airspace, that it had come within 12 miles of the North Korean coast. To refute that claim, NSA, in the days following the shootdown, reported detailed tracking information from radar reflections from Soviet, North Korean,   President Nixon used this NSA-supplied information (and caused some consternation at NSA when reporting the source) to refute the North Korean claim that the aircraft had callously intruded upon its airspace.

Besides the careful study of tracking information, NSA also led the Sigint community in the compilation of a detailed chronology of events before and after the shootdown of the EC-121. Detailing actions by NSA and its field sites in the Far East, NSA officials used this compilation to support and defend the role of Sigint and time-sensitive reporting in the crisis. NSA argued that the field site that played the major role during the shootdown period, [ ] the Air Force Security Service site [ ] performed well in issuing advisory warnings to the aircraft, in trying to determine the fate of the aircraft, and finally in issuing a CRITIC stating the probable shootdown of the plane. [ ] issued this CRITIC nearly an hour after the shootdown. This raised the key question of how quickly the president could be reached in an emergency. In dealing with the CRITIC question, NSA saw the need to remind the military, specifically the Fifth Air Force, that the primary purpose of the CRITIC program was to inform the highest levels of government in Washington of the existence of crisis situations. It was not a vehicle for providing initial alerts to operational commanders so that they could initiate protective actions. With a review of the crisis the Agency proved that the president could indeed be reached quickly in an emergency situation.

Studies of the EC-121 shootdown did show shortcomings in the command and control responsibility for air reconnaissance missions by the military units involved; however, the major problem was the Navy's extremely independent stance in regard to its resources. The Navy was a reluctant participant in an advisory warning program set up by NSA for reconnaissance aircraft. Its planes lacked communications equipment that had become standard on U.S. Air Force planes. This deficiency prevented U.S. officials from determining whether the aircraft received [ ] messages from [ ] A lack of Air Force-Navy communications cooperation also resulted in Navy units in direct control of the aircraft being left off the list of addressees of early warning [ ] reports issued by the Air Force field site. This caused a serious delay in the initiation of search and rescue operations following the shootdown. Military commands also called upon NSA, following the shootdown, to help establish a better system for integrating Sigint intelligence into general intelligence information at military command control centers. Following the crisis, NSA also played an important role in helping the U.S. Air Force establish a Command Advisory Function (CAF) system in which military commands could act more quickly upon information pertaining to reconnaissance missions, and as required, provide protective actions.

In short, NSA played a major role in providing the "whole story" of the shootdown to Washington policymakers.[4] In addition, the shootdown produced a major change in NSA operations. After being called in on the morning of the shootdown, Major General John E. Morrison, Jr., USAF, Assistant Director for Production (ADP), assumed personal direction of the crisis situation at NSA. He immediately had to deal with a number of watch centers to accumulate the necessary data from the Soviet, North Korean, [ ] systems. Although NSA eventually compiled the information, the long journeys around the huge NSA complex that morning convinced Morrison of the need for a focal point for

OGA

EO 1.4.(c)
P.L. 86-36

EO 1.4.(c)
P.L. 86-36

Major General John E. Morrison, Jr. (USAF),
NSA's Assistant Director for Production

3

time-sensitive Sigint information. From this experience evolved the National Sigint Operations Center (NSOC) that remains today a unique capability within the national intelligence community. The EC-121 shootdown crisis represented a conclusive case for convincing Morrison and other NSA decision makers that the full potential of the Sigint system could be realized only through the establishment of a central current operations and crisis-managment center.[5]

BACKGROUND: COLD WAR LEGACY

The forces that collided on 15 April 1969 – the United States Navy reconnaissance plane and the MIG-21s of the North Korean Air Force – were symbols of the Cold War that had developed following World War II. The EC-121 was a part of the Peacetime Aerial Reconnaissance Program (PARPRO) conducted by the United States Navy and Air Force. These programs were developed in the early 1950s as a way of providing intelligence on the Soviet Union and its Communist neighbors. The MIG-21s represented the military forces of a small, hostile Communist nation – North Korea – that itself was a Cold War creation.

The post-World War II years saw the emergence of two major power blocs dominated by two wartime allies – the Western democracies under the leadership of the United States and the Communist nations under the Soviet Union. By 1946, the Cold War had clearly begun. In March of that year, British wartime leader Winston Churchill spoke of an "Iron Curtain" that had dropped across Europe, as he called for an Anglo-American alliance to preserve world order. In June 1947 the Soviets imposed a Communist-dominated government in Hungary and in February 1948 the Communist Party of Czechoslovakia overthrew the elected government of that country. This coup, with the tragic, mysterious death of the popular Czech leader Jan Masaryk, heightened United States' fears of Communist worldwide designs. In early 1947, President Harry S Truman declared that the United States would help any free nation resist Communist aggression. As the U.S. Congress supported the president's request for massive aid to bolster the governments of Greece and Turkey, this Truman Doctrine represented a global pledge by the United States to resist Communist expansion, whether in the form of internal subversion or external aggression. George F. Kennan, then serving on the State Department's new Policy Planning Staff, dubbed it a "policy of containment."[6] Following the establishment of the Communist regime in Czechoslovakia in early 1948, Congress approved the Marshall Plan to carry out a program of aid to Western Europe for economic rehabilitation. This was an effort to assure that a strong, stable Western Europe could resist the spread of communism. Later that year, the United States, Great Britain, and France cooperated in an airlift of supplies into West Berlin when the Soviets carried out a blockade of all ground routes into that city. The capstone of the Truman containment policy in Europe was the decision in 1949 to participate in a North Atlantic Treaty Organization (NATO). This organization committed the United States to defend 10 European countries, from Norway to Italy, against military aggression from the Soviet Union and its satellites.

The announcement in September 1949 that the Soviets had exploded their first atomic bomb produced fears of military inferiority in U.S. policy circles. The United States response to the Cold War drastically changed from economic confrontation to the need to wield strong military force wherever Western interests were threatened.[7] In April 1949 a National Security Council study, NSC-68, presented a pessimistic view of U.S.-Soviet relations to President Truman. The product of a joint State-Defense Department study group under Paul H. Nitze (Kennan's successor as head of State's Policy Planning Staff),

4

included the basic assumption that the Soviet Union was bent on world domination and could neutralize the American atomic advantage by 1954. NSC-68 was even more far-reaching than the Truman Doctrine. It meant that the United States would become a militarized nation, accepting the burdens of a large, permanent military establishment even in peacetime. National security was now defined in global terms with "containment" expanded into a military contest with the Soviets for control of the world. NSC-68 committed the Truman administration to a major struggle with the Soviet Union.[8]

The fall of the Chiang Kai-shek regime to Communist forces under Mao Tse-tung in China followed closely upon the announcement of the first Soviet nuclear test. Another National Security Council policy paper, NSC 48/2, approved by President Truman in December 1949, sought to apply the doctrine of containment of Soviet expansionism to the Far East.[9] In January 1950, Secretary of State Dean Acheson spoke of a "defensive perimeter" of primary importance, including Japan, the Ryukyus, and the Philippines. U.S. policymakers at first rejected a U.S. military defense of the ousted Nationalist Chinese regime in Taiwan and also omitted South Korea from the chain of states to be protected.[10]

The intelligence community's lack of concern over the situation in Korea at that time added to U.S. officials' shock when on 25 June 1950 an invasion force of over 90,000 North Korean troops poured across the 38th parallel into South Korea. In the first months of the Korean War, North Korean troops advanced nearly to the tip of the peninsula before a United Nations contingent of mostly U.S. troops (a Soviet boycott had enabled UN Security Council action) assisted the South Koreans in driving them back across the 38th parallel. The North was saved only by the infusion of hundreds of thousands of Chinese "volunteers" by late 1950. Negotiations for a settlement began as early as July 1951, but the stalemated conflict continued until an armistice agreement was concluded on 27 July 1953.[11] To Truman, as well as the new president, Dwight D. Eisenhower, the intrusion into South Korea and the resulting conflict was a symbol that the Communist nations had passed beyond the use of mere subversion and were now using armed invasion and war to pursue their goal of expansionism.[12]

The administration of Lyndon B. Johnson continued a Cold War policy of containment in Vietnam. To combat guerrilla activity of the Viet Cong in South Vietnam, President Johnson ordered massive bombing of North Vietnam in 1965. The build up of American ground forces shortly followed. The war in Vietnam changed with this American military build up from a local conflict into a struggle between the United States and communism. This reflected a change in the containment policy from one of looking at it strictly in terms of preventing Soviet expansion to one of resisting communism everywhere.[13]

As the United States increasingly committed its military forces to Southeast Asia in the mid and late 1960s, the Communist regime in North Korea exhibited growing hostility toward the United States.[14]

At a Korean Workers' Party Convention in Pyongyang in October 1966, for example, Premier Kim Il-So'ng initiated a campaign of hostile acts aimed at the liberation of South Korea and the unification of the Korean peninsula during his lifetime. A dramatic increase in infiltration efforts into South Korea by small groups of North Korean guerrilla agents began in the autumn of 1966. An initial attack was a predawn raid on the morning of 2 November 1966, in the southern half of the demilitarized zone, that resulted in the death of seven South Korean and American soldiers. The incidents increased tenfold between 1966 and 1967 to over 550 incidents. In 1967, over 125 American and South Korean soldiers were killed in firefights along the DMZ.[15] In 1968, there were over 625 incidents by these infiltration teams. As described by the *New York Times*, it was a "porous war" of terrorist activity.[16] The most daring incident occurred on 21 January 1968, just two days before the USS *Pueblo* was seized by elements of the North

DOCID: 4047116

TOP SECRET UMBRA

Kim Il-So'ng, President of the Democratic People's Republic of Korea

Korean Navy. On that day, 31 infiltrators got within 800 yards of the Blue House, the residence of the South Korean President. The men had come across the DMZ four days earlier with the goal of assassinating South Korean President Chung Hee Park. Although this "Blue House Raid" failed at the last moment, it did not discourage further infiltration attempts. In November 1968, a large group of 120 well-armed and highly trained commando infiltrators landed by sea on the eastern coast of South Korea. This group engaged in Viet Cong-like subversion and sabotage tactics in a number of South Korean villages. It took over 40,000 Republic of Korea militia and policemen nearly two months, with a loss of 63 lives, to clean out this commando group.[17] Although this foray also eventually ended in failure, the dramatic increase in infiltration attempts along the DMZ and the coasts of South Korea represented the attempts of a very hostile North Korean regime to undermine the confidence of the South Korean people in their government. However, the South Korean people showed little sympathy for the infiltrators who had minimal success in establishing guerrilla bases in the south.[18]

In addition to the increase in paramilitary incidents in the late 1960s, North Korea built its regular military, with heavy Soviet aid in equipment and training, into one of the strongest in the Communist world. Between 1966 and 1967, North Korea tripled its defense budget.[19] Military expenditures in North Korea reached 15 to 20 percent of its Gross National Product compared with five percent in South Korea.[20]

By April 1969, the North Korean Army of 350,000 men was the fourth largest in the Communist world. This largely Soviet equipped and trained army was superior to the small American backed South Korean Army.[21] In contrast to the modern North Korean Air Force, for example, the South Korean fighter force of 170 aircraft consisted mainly of the outmoded F-86 Sabre jets.

Despite the superiority of the North Korean military in its training, equipment, and especially air capability, it faced a strong U.S. military presence in the south. The United States military in South Korea had never returned to that nominal pre-Korean War level. By early 1969, over 53,000 U.S. Army troops remained in South Korea as part of the United Nations Command committed to defending the ROK from North Korean aggression. Moreover, in early 1968, the North Koreans seized the U.S. intelligence ship *Pueblo* operating off the Korean coast in international waters.[22]

Between the conclusion of the Korean War and the EC-121 shootdown, the United States and North Korea met 289 times at Panmunjom in the DMZ in their roles as the Military Armistice Commission (MAC), supervising the truce. The two countries did not

TOP SECRET UMBRA and page 6, BODY-11.

BODY-11

disguise their mutual hostility at these meetings which were primarily a forum for exchanging insults and charges. The 289th meeting, for example, held in early April 1969, lasted over 11 hours, with North Korean Major General Ri Choon-sun and U.S. Air Force Major General James B. Knapp, the senior UN delegation member, glaring at each other wordlessly for the final 4-1/2 hours as Knapp waited for Ri to propose a recess.[23] This was the atmosphere in which the U.S. intelligence system operated.

U.S. AERIAL RECONNAISSANCE PROGRAM

To the North Koreans, the Peacetime Aerial Reconnaissance Programs, operated by the United States Air Force and Navy, represented yet another hostile military act and a further deterrent to its aspirations for Korean reunification. These programs were a repercussion of the Cold War atmosphere following World War II and the desire of the United States government to obtain current intelligence on the Soviet Union and other Communist nations. The Airborne Communications Reconnaissance Program (ACRP) of the Air Force Security Service began in the early 1950s in an attempt to deal with changes in the communications practices of the Soviet Union. The Soviets, shortly after the end of World War II, converted their voice communications from high frequency (HF) to very high frequency (VHF) line-of-sight communications. Since these line-of-sight communications could be copied only within 50 to 70 miles of a transmitter, many could not be intercepted by existing U.S. fixed field sites.

On 28 August 1950, General Sam W. Agee at Headquarters USAF gave permission to the USAFSS to develop an airborne intercept program. The potential value of airborne collection was soon shown during the Korean conflict when one VHF intercept position was installed on a Fifth Air Force C-47 aircraft. This effort, known as Project BLUE SKY, was only moderately successful due to poor VHF intercept conditions in the operation area. However, this venture and the testing of RB-29 aircraft in Europe and the Far East convinced Air Force officials of the feasibility of airborne intercept. The RB-29 was assigned to the 6091st Reconnaissance Squadron, Yokota AB, Japan, and flew its first mission in April 1954.[24]

In 1956 budgeting for this airborne reconnaissance activity was increased through the Consolidated Cryptologic Program (CCP), by which the National Security Agency managed all Sigint resources in the National Foreign Intelligence Program (NFIB). The USAFSS dubbed its new program the Airborne Communications Reconnaissance Program (ACRP) in the same year and finalized plans for the use of ten RB-50 aircraft (five each in both Europe and the Far East), as well as the establishment of ACRP detachments in the two theaters to operate the program. The planes were equipped primarily to record voice transmissions in the VHF/UHF range but also included HF, DF (Direction Finding), and CW (continuous-wave or manual Morse) capabilities.

Officials of the National Security Agency quickly recognized the vast potential of this collection system. As the result of successes in the ACRP program in quantity, quality, and uniqueness of the intercept take, NSA officials requested in July 1957 that mission identification data be added to the transcripts of intercepted traffic. The Far East missions were so successful that NSA then requested special missions

By the early 1960s, NSA interest in the ACRP program increased further. The [   ] now possessed the knowledge and equipment to use communication systems as sophisticated as those used by the United States. With the trend [   ] towards using low-powered, directional, and more complex VHF/UHF/microwave transmission,

EO 1.4.(c)
P.L. 86-36

EO 1.4.(c)
P.L. 86-36

NSA experts saw the need to develop an airborne intercept system capable of monitoring these new communication systems. Through NSA sponsored research and development efforts, the C-130s that replaced the RB-50s in the early 1960s were outfitted with updated equipment that greatly increased the ACRP effort against the new ▭ communications systems. This naturally led to an ever increasing interest at both theater and national level in the use of airborne intercept.[26] Airborne collection became increasingly important in meeting demands for intelligence for prior warning of impending military attack on the United States or United States forces overseas. As part of its containment policy, the United States government desired timely intelligence to keep up with Soviet, Chinese Communist North Korean, and Cuban capabilities, intentions, and efforts.

Lieutenant General Gordon A. Blake,
Director of NSA, July 1962 – May 1965

In November 1964, Lieutenant General Gordon A. Blake, USA, Director of NSA, outlined to the Secretary of Defense, Robert S. McNamara, the results of a joint study with the Defense Intelligence Agency (DIA) which addressed the minimum requirements to accomplish the necessary airborne Sigint tasks.[27] A further stimulant to this NSA/DIA study was the problem of United States tenure at some of its base facilities in foreign countries. This threatened to eliminate ground-based collection sites ▭ Blake argued that to fill the void additional airborne resources would be needed. The joint NSA/DIA study concluded that the then current resources of the ACRP fleet (eight C-130A, eleven C-130B, and three RC-135B aircraft) could satisfy ▭ percent of the ▭

OGA

▭ that were deemed necessary to accomplish the Sigint tasks. Airborne collection, the report concluded, was absolutely indispensable in providing unique intelligence on ▭ activities. The NSA/DIA study group recommended that ▭ RC-135Bs be transferred into the ACRP fleet to satisfy most of the stated requirement.[29] As an interim measure, the NSA/DIA team also suggested that the Chief of Naval Operations (CNO), Admiral Thomas H. Moorer, continue using EC-121 aircraft. This aircraft, however, because of its altitude restriction of 9,000 to 16,000 feet (restricting its target penetration capability for peripheral reconnaissance), was not considered as good as the RC-135B for reconnaissance purposes.

In its study of ACRP needs, NSA continued its role as operational and technical director of the Air Force Security Service program. The USAFSS and the other Service Cryptologic Agencies (SCAs) came under the authority of National Security Council Intelligence Directive (NSCID) No. 6. First promulgated in 1952, NSCID No. 6 tasked NSA with producing intelligence as required by the Director of Central Intelligence (DCI)

8

EO 1.4.(c)
P.L. 86-36

and the United States Intelligence Board (USIB).[30] NSA provided the collection (targets and choice of collection facility – including airborne) and technical (time, duration, location, equipment mix, and personnel skills) requirements. The USAFSS managed the collection resources (manpower, aircraft, and equipment) and developed ACRP tracks in coordination with the Air Force theater commands. Theater commands (e.g. CINCPAC – Commander in Chief, Pacific) drew up monthly reconnaissance schedule proposals and forwarded them to the Joint Chiefs of Staff (JCS) for approval and to NSA and USAFSS for information. USAFSS kept NSA advised of its capability to fulfill proposed Sigint collection requirements.

By April 1969 the mission requirements totaled over [   ] The large number in the Far East was due to the growing needs from the Vietnamese conflict. [   ]

To meet the requirements in the Far East, the USAFSS ACRP fleet in the Pacific area consisted of ten C-130B and six RC-135M platforms. The 6988th Security Squadron [   ] manned the 10 C-130s [   ] Eight of the 10, until January 1968, staged out of Yokota AB and Kadena, Okinawa. They flew [   ] orbits as Operation [   ] Following the seizure of the *Pueblo*, two of these planes were reassigned to Osan Air Base, Korea, in response to increased requirements for a predawn/past-dusk early warning service to Fifth Advanced Squadron (Fifth ADVON), 314th Air Division of the Fifth Air Force. This increased collection [   ] was still in effect at the time of the EC-121 shootdown.

The C-130s in the USAFSS ACRP program were solely dedicated to Comint collection, with tasking provided by the National Security Agency. [   ] much of this effort by the early part of 1969 was directed [   ] The USIB desired increased collection activity [   ] in order to evaluate [   ] strength and capabilities.[31]

In contrast to the Air Force ACRP program, in which NSA played a large role in collection requirements and tasking, the Navy program was dedicated largely to fleet support. NSA played only a secondary role in these flights. Two Fleet Air Reconnaissance Squadrons (VQ-1 in the Pacific and VQ-2 in Europe) performed the missions. In 1969 the VQ-1 missions (EC-121M Comint/Elint and EA-3B Elint aircraft) operated from Atsugi, Japan. They were under the direct operational control of the Commander, Seventh Fleet, Admiral William F. Bringle. NSA designated USN-39, the Naval Security Group at [   ] as the responsible station within the cryptologic community for reporting on the [   ] Because of this responsibility and its close proximity to VQ-1, USN-39 manned the Comint positions on the VQ-1 flights.

The NSA tasking role on the VQ-1 flights was a very tenuous one. The Navy jealously guarded its own resources, fearful of any type of NSA control on these flights. The planes were looked upon as Navy assets to be used for carrying out Navy missions.[32] The Navy did permit NSA [   ] tasking on the EC-121 Comint/Elint flights (BEGGAR SHADOW). This [   ] tasking was at the discretion of USN-39 on a "not-to-interfere" basis with the primary requirements of line-of-sight communications [   ] The NSA tasking was updated on 10 March 1969 to avoid duplication with the primary tasking, [   ] Trying to avoid duplication, Eugene Sheck, Chief of K17, the Mobile Collection organization of NSA, faced

OGA

EO 1.4.(c)
P.L. 86-36

~~TOP SECRET UMBRA~~

major difficulties in dealing with the Navy and its reconnaissance missions. He viewed the problem primarily in terms of the Navy's lack of communication with his NSA office. Despite providing this "national tasking" on the two or three flights per month made available by the Navy for that purpose, the Navy usually failed to tell him if and when it was used. Sheck concluded that the Navy often used the NSA tasking as its own.[34] Because of the Navy's failure to communicate, NSA had virtually no voice in the number of flights required, the justification for them, and the risks involved, Sheck complained.

The Navy, according to Sheck, was also a [   ] player" in the [   ] [   ] was the unclassified nickname assigned to JCS procedures and criteria for providing [   ] information to the PARPRO aircraft operating near the periphery of target countries. When aircraft were beyond the range of friendly radar, Sigint sites monitoring [   ] radar networks provided warnings to the aircraft if potentially dangerous conditions (such as approaching enemy fighter aircraft) existed. [   ] Its [   ] response to the JCS [   ] Warning program was also evidenced by its failure to equip its planes with a [   ] secure air-to-ground communications system. The JCS approved this system for [   ] warning purposes in March 1968. By 1969 it was used extensively in the Air Force ACRP program. Sheck cited cost considerations and the failure of the Navy to appreciate the need for the system as reasons for its noninclusion on Navy flights.[35]

Since November 1968, the Navy had directed its BEGGAR SHADOW missions primarily [   ] In response to Seventh Fleet requirements, VQ-1 scheduled two or three EC-121 missions per month [   ] [   ] (After the the *Pueblo* incident and until August 1968, the Joint Chiefs of Staff [   ] (JCS [   ] restricted the flights to at least 80 miles off the [   ] coast.) The Navy flew these new tracks 14 times from November 1968 to April 1969; the 15th was the ill-fated mission of 15 April 1969. Elint tasking was provided by fleet or theater sources, and final schedules approved by theater Elint planning conferences. The schedule, after final approval by the Theater Command (CINCPAC), was forwarded to DIA for review, before being finally presented to the JCS/JRC. At the time the NSA role in the Elint flights under [   ] was limited to a technical review conducted by the K4 element.[37] NSA's only responsibility was to ensure that specific mission aircraft possessed the technical collection capability to meet requirements. NSA issued no supplemental Elint tasking applicable to these BEGGAR SHADOW missions.

Since the BEGGAR SHADOW flights were primarily Elint oriented [   ] [   ] NSA (B Group) provided no Sigint tasking on these missions. The VQ-1 flights, therefore, provided only a small amount of intelligence to the Agency and this was usually duplicative in nature.[38] The main value of the flights was in providing information on the

[   ]

The minimal NSA role on these Navy missions, its limitation to a "technical review" status, was closely related to the overall fragmented management of United States Elint resources. NSA officials viewed the Elint program as one lacking coordination, thus causing gross duplication and waste. In theory, NSA's authority (as specified in NSCID No. 6) in Elint was almost identical to its authority in Comint. However, a serious loophole existed in Department of Defense Directive No. 3115-2. This directive gave

OGA

EO 1.4.(c)
P.L. 86-36

military commanders the responsibility to collect and process Elint determined necessary for direct support activities in conducting electronic measures and countermeasures (such as radar jamming, the use of chaff, and other deceptive devices) in military operations. Using this loophole, the services, including the Navy, interpreted electronic countermeasures to cover almost any kind of Elint activity. In contrast, Directive No. 3115-4, dealing with Comint, was much more precise in defining activities exempted from NSA control. NSA officials, such as Arthur J. Levenson, Chief of A Group, viewed the establishment of Comint-like rules as necessary to combat the current fragmented state of Elint. As satellite reconnaissance played a more important role in intercept, and with NSA heavily involved in the planning and operation of such systems, Levenson saw the need for a more active role in reviewing this expensive airborne Elint program to reduce duplication of effort.[39] Pressure for this review mounted as the EC-121 continued its mission.

The EC-121 flight of 15 April characterized the Navy autonomy. Although the Navy called it a BEGGAR SHADOW mission, thus implying a primary Comint role (with national tasking), its role on that flight was virtually limited to that of an Elint-only operation. (While this EC-121 flight was always referred to as a BEGGAR SHADOW mission, a SAC message of 26 April 1969 referred to it as the [   ] which was more appropriate as it was the nickname referring to direct support Elint flights.)[40] In fact, even the make-up of the large crew on this flight reflected this. Ten members of the crew held the title of Aviation Electronic Technician, signifying them as electronic countermeasures personnel, and thus outside of NSA's Sigint authority. On the ill-fated flight they outnumbered the communications technicians, Sigint personnel assigned to Naval Security Group at [   ] NSA's passive role relating to these flights added to the confusion at Fort Meade on the morning of the shootdown as questions arose over who controlled the aircraft, who tasked the mission, and what it was trying to collect. Even CINCPACFLT, which was in the immediate chain of command of the aircraft, issued seemingly conflicting statements regarding the primary mission of the flight. A CINCPACFLT message of 1 April 1969, for example, gave the proposed VQ-1 EC-121 schedule for April. This message listed Comint as the primary task of the EC-121 missions, Elint as a secondary task. However, on 16 April (the day after the shootdown), CINCPACFLT described BEGGAR SHADOW Track 8263 (the track of the ill-fated mission) as designed to optimize Elint collection [   ] A DIA memorandum of 18 April further described four EC-121 tracks (including 8263) flown since November 1968 as meeting theater requirements under the [   ] Elint program. Track 8263 had been flown four times earlier in 1969 as had a similar track, 8261. These tracks were designed primarily to provide intelligence on North Korean radar activities.[41] NSA levied no special supplemental Elint tasking that was applicable to the mission.[42]

THE RISK ASSESSMENT PROCESS

In addition to its minimal tasking role, NSA did not participate in the risk assessment process (to establish the likelihood of enemy hostile actions) on these Navy flights. During the 20-year period dating back to 1950, U.S. reconnaissance aircraft were subject to enemy attacks on over 40 occasions. Most of these incidents, in which the United States lost 16 aircraft, were attributed to the Soviet Union. On occasion, however, the North Koreans attacked United States reconnaissance vehicles. One incident occurred just after the armistice concluding the Korean conflict. North Korean antiaircraft fire in August 1953 shot down a USAF T-6 intelligence mission over the DMZ. Six years later, the North Koreans attacked a U.S. Navy reconnaissance flight. The Martin P4M-1Q Mercator,

11

EO 1.4.(c)
P.L. 86-36

originally designed as a long-range bomber, had been modified in the late 1950s to take on a new role in electronic reconnaissance. A number of these served the VQ-1 and VQ-2 squadrons. On 16 July 1959, two North Korean MIGs shot at an Elint Mercator flight. The incident occurred at 7,000 feet over international waters, nearly 40 miles off the Korean coast. The Mercator managed to escape by diving to sea level and badly damaged, with a wounded tailgunner, limped back to a forced landing on a Japanese airfield.[43] On 27 April 1965, North Korean MIG-17s from So'ndo'k attacked and badly damaged another Elint mission, an Air Force RB-47, over the Sea of Japan, 80 miles off the coast.

The seizure of the USS *Pueblo* on 23 January 1968 brought to a climax this series of occasional attacks on elements of United States intelligence forces. Originally a U.S. Army supply ship in the Pacific from 1944–54, the *Pueblo* was reactivated and turned over to the Navy in 1966. It was converted to an Auxiliary General Environmental Research (AGER) vessel as a result of an urgent request by the Secretary of the Navy, Paul H. Nitze. Nitze also asked for two more trawler vessels to augment the tactical surveillance and intelligence collection capability⬛

While the USS *Pueblo*, under Lieutenant Commander Lloyd M. Bucher, was undergoing its final mission preparations in December 1967, the National Security Agency issued a warning about North Korean dangers. In a message dated 29 December 1967 to the⬛

Sent to aid in the JCS-CINCPAC risk assessment process, the message cited the downing of the USAF RB-47 in April 1965 as an example of this North Korean sensitivity. The item further cited recent reactions by the North Korean Navy to South Korean Navy vessels and even fishing vessels near the North Korean coastline. These included the sinking of a South Korean naval vessel on 19 January 1967 by coastal artillery.[44]

The NSA message sent during the height of the holiday season was virtually ignored. It was routed as routine information to CINCPAC and not seen by Admiral U.S. Grant Sharp until after the capture of the *Pueblo*.[45] The seizure of the ship by a subchaser and torpedo boats of the North Korean Navy occurred 12 days after the *Pueblo* had departed from Sasebo harbor on its first (and only) intelligence mission.

The *Pueblo* seizure was certainly a major reason for increased United States intelligence efforts against North Korea. The incident was still under investigation by a congressional subcommittee as Lieutenant Commander James H. Overstreet met with other members of an EC-121 crew for a preflight briefing. The routine briefing did contain a warning. Overstreet discussed three messages in the briefing including one from the Commander of U.S. Forces in Korea, General Charles H. Bonesteel III, to CINCPAC (Admiral John S. McCain, Jr.) on 11 April 1969.[46] This message warned of unusually vehement and vicious language used by the North Koreans in recent Military Armistice Commission meetings held at Panmunjom. Although this communication was especially directed to crews of⬛the VQ-1 squadron was told to be alert and be prepared to abort at the first indication of any serious reactions by the North Koreans.[47] Despite these warnings, neither the Seventh Fleet nor CINCPAC made an attempt to change the⬛which

⬛In fact, this flight track was reviewed by Seventh Fleet on 14 April with no basis seen for an⬛[48] As a precaution, however, the flight was to approach no closer than 50 miles to the Korean coast.[49]

While Commander Overstreet and other members of the EC-121 crew prepared for their mission, they were unaware of the unusual activity at an airfield on North Korea's east coast. Hoemun was the home base of the North Korean Air Force (NKAF) Air

OGA

School's Jet Training Element. While this element was normally equipped only with MIG-15/17 aircraft, two NKAF First Fighter Division MIG-21 (Fishbed-F) aircraft flew to Hoemun on 28 March from Pukch'ang-ni Airfield.[50] The Joint Sobe Processing Center (JSPC), located at Torii Station, Okinawa, sent a message on 30 March 1969 to all Far East military commands and Sigint sites which indicated that this first reflection of Fishbed-F type aircraft at Hoemun was probably related to pilot training since a MIG-21 Transition Training Unit was located at another east coast location, Pukch'ang-ni.[51] There was no known NKAF tactical unit located at Hoemun. On the morning of 15 April, the two MIG-21s remained at Hoemun. Such was the initial warning of the coming crisis.

MIG-21 Fishbed F fighter, shown here with insignia of the Czech Air Force.

THE SHOOTDOWN

The BEGGAR SHADOW mission, assigned [   ] and [   ] [   ] took off from Atsugi Naval Air Station, Japan, at 0700 local time (2200Z)[52] with 31 men on board. The scheduled flight duration was eight and a half hours. From Atsugi, the EC-121 was to fly to a point off the northeastern coastal city of Ch'ongjin, near North Korea's border with Manchuria. The plane was then to fly two and a half orbits along a 120 mile elliptical path parallel to the coast of North Korea before continuing to Osan AB, near Seoul, with a projected arrival time of 0630Z. Except for the beginning and ending legs over Japan and South Korea, the entire flight was to be over international waters. It was to fly no closer than 50 miles to the North Korean coast (see map 1). The North Koreans claimed territorial waters and airspace 12 miles from their coast.

OGA

13

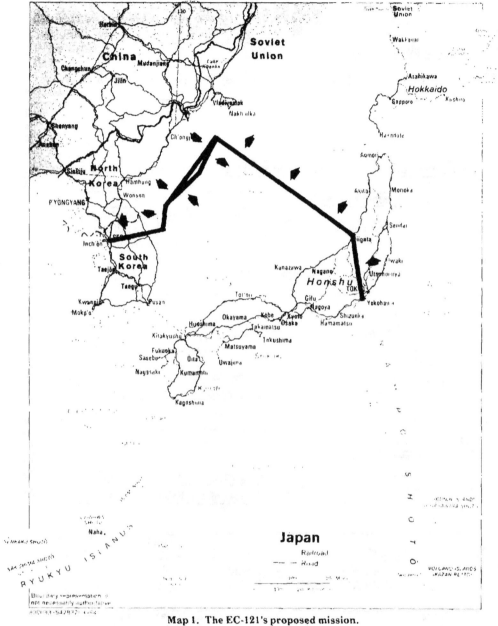

Map 1. The EC-121's proposed mission.
Its schedule included take off from Atsugi Naval Air Station, Japan, performing two
and a half orbits off the coast of North Korea (at an approach not to exceed 50 nautical
miles) and landing at Osan, Republic of Korea, approximately eight and a half hours
after departure.

14

EO 1.4.(c)
P.L. 86-36

EC-121, "slow and lumbering," was a modification of a plane that was once a familiar sight to transatlantic air travelers: the Lockheed Super Constellation, a major commercial plane before the jet age. The plane's four propeller-driven engines provided a maximum speed of 220 knots with a maximum altitude of 10,000 to 20,000 feet. The unarmed aircraft carried nearly six tons of electronic equipment with a bulbous radome on top to pick up radar signals and antennas under the plane's belly to monitor radio communications. The plane contained

A

communications position included secure voice (KY-8) and secure teletype (KW-7) equipment.[53]

OGA

Friendly radar coverage would be available during part of the flight from Japan and South Korea. part of the flight the plane would be dependent upon

Before each flight the Navy provided complete flight path and times to Specific areas of responsibility for warning were designated the airborne collector proceeded along its flight path.[54]

One of the Sigint sites that provided support on the EC-121 flight was the designator for the

Its role in the flight of the EC-121 was to cover trackings of the flight and to coordinate via operational communications (OPSCOMM) circuitry with USA-58.[55]

USA-58, the Sigint designator for the 6918th Security Squadron of the USAFSS, was a cotenant at the U.S. Army Security Station at Hakata, Kyushu, Japan. For the EC-121 flight, it was to provide coverage and to act as a relay

The key role in the entire episode was played by

This unit's primary responsibility was collecting information Since most of the EC-121 flight

information was also to be passed to appropriate command and control facilities for possible action, such as a fighter launch. In the case of such a launch, was to contact units of the Fifth Air Force, the Fifth ADVON, and the 314th Air Division, located at Osan, through secure voice and teletype.[56]

USN-39, the Naval Security Group facility at Kamiseya, Japan, was to serve as another relay point in the Sigint network, but communications problems would put it out of the picture until well after the shootdown occurred.[57] Because of its proximity to VQ-1, it had control over manning the onboard positions of the EC-121 flight.

Following its 0700 (2200Z 14 April) takeoff from the Atsugi Naval Air Station near Tokyo, the crew of the EC-121 was in direct contact with Kamiseya, during the

The EC-121 was a modified Lockheed Super Constellation, a four-engine plane that flew most major commercial airline routes before the introduction of jets.

BODY-21

early hours of the flight. At the very beginning of the mission (2217Z) Commander Overstreet called Kamiseya for a ground check. This was receipted by USN-39 several minutes later. An hour and a half later (2347Z), chatter took place between the plane and USN-39 in an attempt to correct some minor communications difficulties. These problems were cleared up by 0025Z. Twenty minutes later the last direct contact occurred between the plane and Kamiseya. At that time (0045Z), the crew had some activity on a radio-telephone position and informed USN-39 that no further transmissions would be forthcoming while this took place. The reason for this action was to prevent the loss of intercept which sometimes occurred during KW-7 transmissions. The plane would simply acknowledge any transmissions from the ground by sending three short sync pulses on the KW-7 circuit.[58]

Osan, via OPSCOMM from USA-58, Hakata, was made aware at 0008Z of the departure of the Navy mission. The initial reflection of the flight – BEGGAR SHADOW

The plane, was initially reflected over the Sea of Japan at 0105Z approximately 150 nm southeast of Vladivostok.[59] informed of this Soviet reaction at 0117Z.[60] The EC-121 continued on a northwesterly path to a point about 90 nm southeast of Vladivostok (also representing the closest point to Soviet territory at 60 nm)

A few minutes prior to this (0125Z), the aircraft receipted with sync pulses in response to USN-39 communications

Shortly after 0300Z, as the EC-121 again routinely acknowledged an hourly communications check, later carefully studied at NSA headquarters, occurred as the plane made its closest approach to the North Korean landmass. Later used by NSA to repudiate claims of the North Koreans that the plane had violated its airspace,

USA-58, were unable to assist at this critical point. USA-58, Hakata, informed Osan that it was reflecting an Air Force ACRP mission in the Vladivostok Bay area, but not the EC-121. In fact, tracking was extremely sparse after its initial reflections several hours before. Unable to glean any information from these other sites, decided against issuing a warning to the EC-121 at the time. At 0315Z it informed

EO 1.4.(c)
P.L. 86-36

EO 1.4.(c)
P.L. 86-36

Shortly thereafter the plane began its long elliptical orbit to the southwest. At 0319Z, USA-58 informed Osan that [____] had no [____] reflections of the plane. At that point [____] lost contact with USA-58 when its OPSCOMM circuit went out for about 19 minutes. [_____] However, [_____] continued to reflect the plane throughout the next crucial hour (see map 3). The [____] [____] tracking was now more compatible with the expected path of the EC-121. The OPSCOMM circuit with Hakata was restored at 0334Z. Osan now seemed convinced that it was reflecting the "Navy Bird," Track 8263. While reflecting the EC-121 at the beginning of this elliptical orbit, [____] also reported to Hakata that it had tracked fighters over the water at 0329Z. The fighter reflections, however, were far to the southwest, over the Tongjo-son Bay, and seemed nonthreatening. USA-58 still had no reflections of the aircraft or any indication of possible hostile activity. By 0344Z [____] reported the fighters as heading back toward the Korean landmass. For the next half hour, the U.S. reconnaissance plane continued on its southwest leg, reaching the southernmost point of the orbit area at about 0400Z. The [_____] USA-58 OPSCOMM circuit was quiet.[64]

As the EC-121 approached the southern limit of its elliptical track the final transmission from the plane occurred. Shortly after 0400Z it responded to the hourly communications check by [_____] Kamiseya. It was still being tracked by [_____] [____] radar and still reflected a course compatible with the planned flight route. The [_____]

[_____] Communications between [_____] USA-58 were reestablished at 0420Z. At the same time [____] reported it had picked up fighter reactions again, this time over the Sea of Japan, over 100 miles east of Hoemun. [_____]

As the EC-121 approached the northern part of the elliptical orbit at 0430Z, the two MIG-21s that had appeared at the Hoemun Air School in late March took off across the waters of the Sea of Japan in what appeared to be a carefully calculated maneuver.[65] In retrospect, the planes were scrambled at a time that allowed minimum flight time over water for intercept of a plane that was flying on a previously known reconnaissance track. During the next several minutes [____] had to take decisive action. There was no time to coordinate information with the other sites. The Korean fighters were moving rapidly across the Sea of Japan. The initial reflections of the MIG-21s were picked up at 0435Z at [_____] [_____] supervisor decided to wait for a second plotting to determine the validity of the tracking before taking any action. Within two minutes he determined that the fighters were reflected within 51 to 55 nm of the EC-121 which itself was reflected as heading away from the fighters on an easterly turn across the Sea of Japan.[67]

At 0438Z, the [____] supervisor at [_____] [_____]

[_____] (The [____] system was standard equipment in aircraft of the Air Force ACRP fleet.) In the Air Force planes, advisory

OGA

EO 1.4.(c)
P.L. 86-36

EO 1.4.(c)
P.L. 86-36

BODY-25

EO 1.4.(c)
P.L. 86-36

warnings were automatically receipted for in the form of a data burst transmission that set off a light on a ground console. In the Navy plane, ⬛⬛⬛⬛⬛⬛⬛⬛⬛⬛⬛ (a series of numbers), which was done in a remarkably fast manner, but was still slower than in the automatic ⬛⬛⬛⬛ system. ⬛⬛⬛⬛ [88]

Within the next 10 minutes ⬛⬛ at 0440Z, just two minutes after the ⬛⬛⬛⬛⬛⬛⬛⬛⬛⬛⬛⬛⬛⬛⬛⬛⬛⬛⬛⬛⬛ followed at 0448Z due to the possibility that there was an additional fighter reaction. ⬛⬛⬛⬛⬛⬛⬛⬛⬛⬛⬛⬛⬛⬛⬛⬛⬛⬛⬛⬛⬛⬛⬛⬛⬛⬛⬛⬛⬛⬛⬛⬛⬛⬛⬛⬛⬛ By that time the MIG-21 had reached the EC-121. ⬛⬛⬛⬛⬛⬛⬛⬛⬛⬛⬛⬛⬛⬛⬛⬛⬛⬛⬛⬛ One of the jets from Hoemun Air Field performed a defensive patrol over the Sea of Japan, with a position 65 nm west of the EC-121 at the closest approach. The other jet continued on an eastward track and ⬛⬛⬛⬛⬛⬛⬛⬛ noted the merging of its track and that of the EC-121 at 0444Z (see map 4). The time of the shootdown was probably 0447Z, approximately 80 miles west of the North Korean coast (41-12N, 131-48E). The ⬛⬛⬛⬛⬛⬛⬛⬛ noted the separation of the tracks at 0449Z, and by 0451Z ⬛⬛⬛⬛⬛⬛⬛⬛⬛⬛⬛⬛⬛⬛⬛ ceased to reflect the EC-121. However, ⬛⬛⬛⬛⬛⬛⬛⬛⬛⬛⬛⬛⬛⬛⬛⬛ continued to reflect the fighters until 0507Z as they headed west over the Sea of Japan back toward Hoemun.

In addition to passing ⬛⬛⬛⬛⬛⬛⬛⬛⬛⬛ information to the aircraft, ⬛⬛⬛⬛ also ⬛⬛⬛⬛⬛⬛⬛⬛⬛⬛⬛⬛⬛⬛⬛⬛⬛⬛⬛⬛⬛⬛⬛⬛⬛⬛⬛⬛ From the time of the ⬛⬛⬛⬛⬛⬛⬛⬛⬛⬛⬛⬛⬛⬛⬛⬛⬛⬛⬛ with the Fifth AF ADVON, Osan, ⬛⬛⬛⬛⬛⬛⬛⬛⬛⬛⬛⬛⬛⬛ Warning Center (Osan) via OPSCOMM. This was to permit operational actions to be taken by the commanders concerned. ⬛⬛⬛⬛⬛⬛⬛⬛⬛⬛⬛⬛⬛⬛⬛⬛⬛ by OPSCOMM to USA-58 for relay to the Fifth Air Force.[69] At 0442Z an OPSCOMM direct service tip-off was sent to the 314th Air Division Warning Center, and several minutes later ⬛⬛⬛⬛ issued an initial SPOT report that two KORCOM fighters ⬛⬛⬛⬛⬛⬛⬛⬛⬛⬛⬛⬛⬛⬛⬛⬛⬛⬛⬛⬛⬛⬛ were probably reacting to the BEGGAR SHADOW mission. ⬛⬛⬛ directed this SPOT report to 43 addressees (Hotel Six/Foxtrot was the distribution designator) but not VQ-1 or USN-39, the commands directly responsible for operation and Comint manning of the aircraft.[70] This oversight would later be cited in Congressional hearings as an example of the Command Control breakdown that existed during the shootdown. Although the specific cause for this lapse was never revealed, it certainly represented a lack of communication between the Navy units directly responsible for the plane (VQ-1, USN-39) and the USAFSS field site responsible for Sigint information ⬛⬛⬛⬛⬛ At 0451Z, ⬛⬛⬛⬛⬛ sent a follow-up to the direct service tip-off to the 314th Air Division citing the merged positions of the EC-121 and a fighter aircraft at 0447Z, the probable shootdown time.

When Brigadier General Arthur W. Holderness, Commander of the 314th Air Division at Osan, became aware of the tip-off ⬛⬛⬛⬛⬛⬛⬛ of fighter reaction to the flight at 0445Z, he immediately ordered the launch of two F-102s to be placed on a CAP (Combat Air Patrol) orbit 140 nm off the South Korean coastal city of Kangnung, around 100 nm south of the incident area. This was in the vicinity of the planned flight path of the EC-121 as it headed on its final leg to Osan. The F-102s were to proceed to this area to search for the EC-121 and to rescue it from harassment or attack if it was still in flight.

OGA

EO 1.4.(c)
P.L. 86-36

EO 1.4.(c)
P.L. 86-36

BODY-27

EO 1.4.(c)
P.L. 86-36

Unfortunately, the launch time of 0504Z occurred about 17 minutes after the 0447Z assumed shootdown time of the EC-121. The Fifth Air Force Headquarters in Japan was still unaware of the seriousness of the situation. It asked [   ] to query [   ] [ ] why the Commander of 314th Air Division (General Holderness) scrambled two fighters in Combat Air Patrol.

OGA

[blank box]

While the F-102s looked for the reconnaissance mission off the South Korean coast, the U.S. Sigint field sites spent a hectic hour trying to determine the fate of the EC-121. At 0500Z USN-39 made its usual hourly communications check with the aircraft. This time there was no response. From 0505Z to 0612Z, USN-39 made nine more unsuccessful attempts to contact the plane. Despite the lack of a response, there was no unusual concern as USN-39 personnel were not aware of the warnings and reports initiated by [   ] due to being left off the distribution. The failure of the plane to respond was not considered unusual due to the distance involved and the fact that communications between aircraft and Kamiseya were often mediocre at best.[73] At VQ-1, Atsugi, an Air Plot Duty Officer had copied the [   ] warning messages sent from the station at Fuchu. Aware that the possibility of a problem existed, VQ-1 made a number of calls to Fuchu over the next half-hour for any communications from the mission aircraft and requested that all sources be checked for a possible abort message. At 0558Z VQ-1 sent a FLASH message to [   ] USA-58 requesting any information on reflections of the flight.

OGA

After issuing its initial SPOT report at 0445Z, [   ] spent the next hour in an intensified effort to locate the mission aircraft. This included replotting of tracking information, [   ] and extensive coordination with other sites (Fifth ADVON/314th Air Division, USA-58, [   ] [   ] requested USA-58, Hakata, at 0500Z to check with [   ] and the Fifth Air Force to see if they had anything on the aircraft, stating "Mate, has anyone had any tracking on that BEGGAR SHADOW since 0447Z?"[74] By 0515Z [   ] had confirmed that tracking of the fighters had ceased about 0504Z. Captain [   ] the commanding officer of [   ] then queried the Special Security Officer of the nearby 314th Air Division to see if it had any communications with the plane and whether the plane was still to land at Osan. The 314th Air Division advised that it was probable that the plane had received the warnings [   ] taken evasive action on its eastward turn, and could have "hit the deck" (dropped below radar cover). As the plane returned south, however, it should have been reflected by friendly radar and communications reestablished.[75] At 0520Z, [   ] issued a second follow-up to its SPOT report, advising that there had been no further reflections of the BEGGAR SHADOW mission since 0447Z. Again, the Hotel Six/Foxtrot address eliminated receipt of this information by [   ] or VQ-1.[76]

EO 1.4.(c)
EO 1.4.(d)
P.L. 86-36

P.L. 86-36

[blank box]

EO 1.4.(c)
P.L. 86-36

While still trying to determine the meaning [REDACTED] decided to go ahead with the issuance of a CRITIC. During the contact with [REDACTED] regarding the [REDACTED] had been advised that it was probably best to issue a CRITIC. All was not well. In addition, in replotting [REDACTED] confirmed that the Korean fighter tracks did indeed merge with that of the EC-121. At 0544Z [REDACTED] issued a CRITIC to DIRNSA stating that [REDACTED] reflected the possible shootdown of the BEGGAR SHADOW over the Sea of Japan at approximately 0447Z.[78] The original CRITIC was addressed only to NSA. It overrode all other material in the Critical Intelligence Communications Network (CRITICOMM). Immediately upon its arrival at NSA it was retransmitted to the White House and to a number of other high-level Washington addressees. In addition, after the originator issued the CRITIC, the same text was addressed in a Lateral CRITIC to a special worldwide distribution.[79]

This Lateral CRITIC was addressed to a Hotel Six/Zulu distribution. USN-39, Kamiseya, was included as an addressee in this distribution and received the CRITIC via OPSCOMM at 0558Z. This was the first indication USN-39 had of a possible shootdown. Kamiseya quickly passed the item to VQ-1 which had just minutes before sent out its FLASH message requesting information on reflections of the mission. Fifty-seven minutes elapsed between the shootdown (0447Z) and the CRITIC issuance (0544Z). (This time gap became a controversial point in the days ahead. NSA played a major role in coming to the defense of the intelligence community, specifically in defending the actions of [REDACTED]

As the expected arrival time of the EC-121 at Osan (0630Z) came and passed, U.S. officials became convinced that the plane was lost. Within the hour, reports of a radio broadcast from Pyongyang further substantiated these fears. The Foreign Broadcast Information Service (FBIS) reported that at 0655Z a North Korean language broadcast from the Pyongyang Domestic Service announced the shootdown of a U.S. reconnaissance plane at 0450Z when it "intruded" into Korean airspace.[80] Shortly after, at 0800Z, the FBIS monitored a North Korean Central News Agency report in English. The shootdown was further described as a "brilliant achievement" by the North Korean Air Force in downing "with one stroke at a high altitude" a reconnaissance plane of the "U.S. imperialist aggressor troops." Any retaliation, it was further announced, would be met with "hundredfold revenge."[81]

SEARCH AND RESCUE OPERATIONS

Although the 314th Air Division scrambled fighters within 17 minutes after receiving an alert from [REDACTED] no unit initiated search and rescue operations for over an hour after the shootdown.[82] This did not occur until VQ-1, the operating unit of the EC-121, learned of the probable shootdown from the Lateral CRITIC received at USN-39 at 0601Z. Within 10 minutes, VQ-1 contacted the Fifth Air Force Combat Operations Center at Fuchu and requested the initiation of search and rescue operations.[83] By 0644Z, the Fifth Air Force informed VQ-1 that an HC-130 was airborne from Tachikawa Air Base, outside of Tokyo,

EO 1.4.(c)
P.L. 86-36

with F-106 fighters scrambled from South Korea to serve as a CAP. By the time the HC-130 reached the shootdown area several hours later, daylight was coming to an end. An initial report from the HC-130 of smoke flares and multiple survival beacons provided some early hope that there were survivors. Shortly thereafter, however, the first report was deemed erroneous. The smoke flares were dropped by rescue aircraft and the beacons were found to be onboard the rescue aircraft.[84] Vice Admiral William F. Bringle, Commander of the Seventh Fleet, on board the USS *Oklahoma* off South Vietnam when informed by VQ-1 of the [____] CRITIC, directed the vessels *Dale* and *Tucker*, located at Sasebo, Japan, to proceed to the area of the shootdown. They departed Sasebo about 1300Z.

An interesting aspect of the search and rescue operations was the participation of the Soviet Union. At the time of the shootdown, a Soviet Ugra submarine tender (#945) with two Foxtrot-class submarines were in the immediate area. Later, three Soviet destroyers moved into the area as well. With the Soviet vessels so close, Washington appealed to the Soviet government to help locate any survivors. U.S. Ambassador James D. Beam, in Moscow, asked the head of the USA section of the Soviet Foreign Ministry, Georgi M. Kornienko for aid. Kornienko stated he had no knowledge of the incident or of the missing aircraft but would inform his government of the American request.[85] In Washington, Secretary of State William P. Rogers called Soviet ambassador Anatoly F. Dobrynin into his office shortly after noon to discuss the shootdown. Rogers stated that the American plane had not violated North Korean airspace and that the United States was unsure at this point if there were any survivors. Rogers then repeated the U.S. request expressed earlier in Moscow that the Soviet ships in the shootdown area assist in the rescue of possible survivors.[86] In line with this desire for Soviet aid, the Joint Chiefs of Staff directed U.S. forces operating in the Sea of Japan not to interfere with rescue attempts by other ships, regardless of nationality. Also, the Fifth Air Force ordered [____] not to issue any [_____] on Soviet aircraft in the vicinity of search and rescue operations.

The first hard evidence of the shootdown was the spotting of debris by a Navy P-3 rescue plane on the morning of 16 April at 41-14N/131-50E, two nm northeast of the reported shootdown location. This debris consisted of uninflated life rafts and paper and dye markers. The Soviet role in the search operations began later that day when the rescue aircraft made contact with two Soviet ships in the shootdown area. These were the Soviet destroyers DD429 and DD580. That afternoon, aided by the American rescue aircraft personnel who dropped identifying smoke bombs, the destroyers began to pick up debris from the aircraft. To further aid in the joint effort, the United States launched an HC-130 from Osan with a Russian-speaking crew member on board. Radio contact with one Soviet ship (DD580) revealed that pieces of the plane had been picked up, but that there was no sign of any survivors. The Soviets granted permission for an American plane to fly low over the ship to photograph the debris. A URC-10 survival radio was also dropped to Soviet ships in order to establish communications. In the early evening two U.S. ships arrived in the area, the destroyer *Henry W. Tucker* and the missile frigate USS *Dale*.[87]

OGA

There were no survivors. On the following morning, 17 April, the waters of the Sea of Japan yielded two bodies from the ill-fated mission. The victims were identified as Lieutenant (j.g.) Joseph R. Ribar and AT1 Richard E. Sweeney. They were the only bodies recovered of the 31 men on board and were found about 17 nm north of the general shootdown area. Winds and currents continued to cause the northward drift of the debris throughout the day to the vicinity of the North Korean and Soviet coasts. Soviet aid was again requested – to pick up any bodies or debris within 20 nm of the coastlines.[88] The

25

search operation continued throughout the day with the two destroyers, one HC-130, one P-3, and four F-106s on CAP by the Fifth Air Force.

On 18 April, the *Tucker* rendezvoused with the Soviet destroyer *Vodokhnovenny* (DD429) to receive debris recovered by the Soviet ship during the search. Included in the transfer was the radio dropped to the Soviet ship by the USAF rescue aircraft, a 20-man life boat, three leather jackets, a parachute, two exposure suits, and some aircraft parts. The *Tucker* then proceeded to Sasebo, Japan, with the bodies of the two crewmen recovered and over 500 pounds of debris.[89]

The Joint Chiefs of Staff officially terminated the search and rescue operations at 2036Z on 19 April. No North Korean ships were sighted during the search and rescue exercise and no classified material was in the exchange of debris from the Soviet destroyer DD429 to the USS *Tucker*. However, a few pieces of classified material were recovered by the *Dale* and *Tucker*. These included a piece of the bulkhead containing the crew's positions, a radar antenna, a photograph ░░░░░░░░░ pages of a computer printout ░░░░░░░░ and several pages of handwritten operator's notes found in the personal effects of Richard Sweeney.[90] Among the classified material considered lost or compromised were ░░░░░░░░░░░░░░░░░░░░

░░░░░░░░░░[91]

OGA

1.4.(c)
P.L. 86-36

From the wreckage recovered from the Sea of Japan a joint U.S. Navy-Air Force investigative team concluded that the EC-121 sustained major structural damage from the detonation of a fragmenting warhead of one (or possibly two) air-to-air missiles. It was probably of the infrared, heat-seeking (ATOLL) type – an exact copy of the U.S. Sidewinder Missile.[92]

NSA REACTION

As ░░░░░ desperately tried to assess the fate of the EC-121 mission on that April afternoon, a small number of employees at the National Security Agency headquarters reported in on their midnight shift. One group reported to the Current Sigint Operations Center (CSOC), established in 1967 as a mechanism for Sigint surveillance and reporting on A group targets – ░░░░░░░░░░░░░░░░░░░░░░░░░ The Senior Operations Officer was ░░░░░░░░░░░ A811. A routine Tuesday morning was soon ended with a call from ░░░░░ Hakata, reporting that it was acting as a relay for ░░░░░ which had a problem. ░░ was also trying to decide whether to send out a CRITIC on the possible shootdown of the plane. While unable to help on the ░░░░░ ░░░░░ recommended immediate issuance of the CRITIC by ░░░░░ This CRITIC was received by OPSCOMM at CSOC at 0550Z (0050 EST). Immediately upon receipt of the CRITIC, CSOC personnel began to gather and plot ░░░░░ tracking data. They requested that ░░░░░ send all of its tracking data to headquarters and that it be informed of any ░░░░░ follow-up actions.

P.L. 86-36

Another NSA unit involved in the early morning crisis was the Command Center. Essentially a 24-hour watch-type element for the Production Organization, it had been in existence since 1963. Approximately 25 persons, including representatives from A, B, G, and P organizations were on duty, with ░░░░░░░░░░ as the Senior Operations

EO 1.4.(c)
P.L. 86-36

P.L. 86-36
EO 1.4.(c)

TOP SECRET UMBRA

P.L. 86-36

Officer.[94] Receiving an early morning query from [   ] about receipt of a CRITIC from [   ] [   ] recognized the development of another crisis situation and called Major General John E. Morrison, Jr., the Assistant Director for Production (ADP). Morrison was summoned to assume personal direction of the situation. He arrived at the Command Center shortly after 0200 hours. On Morrison's advice calls were also made to Lieutenant General Marshall S. Carter, the Director, NSA, and Louis W. Tordella, the Deputy Director.[95] Morrison also advised calling in [   ] Chief, B1, who was responsible for the North Korean problem.

The Command Center notified the B Watch Office of Morrison's request. Unlike the large A Group CSOC operation, the B watch was small and had no reporting capability. The watch quickly began to call in key B Group personnel, however, including John Apollony, B05, and Carl A. Miller and [   ] of B11, as well as [ ] Meanwhile, Morrison called Eugene Sheck of K17, the [   ] organization, for answers relating to this Navy flight.

By 0300 hours, [   ] and Sheck had joined Morrison in the Command Center. At first they assumed a maximum flight crew of 15 persons. However, Sheck informed Morrison that this figure could very well be doubled. The number of personnel on these flights, he said, was sometimes doubled for training purposes or to provide liberty for the extra men. Morrison appeared uneasy. Thirty men could be lost on this mission.[96] Besides dealing with an incident involving an overloaded aircraft Morrison had major doubts concerning the plane being in that area in the first place. Despite the BEGGAR SHADOW appellation, the flight was strictly a Navy direct-support flight which Morrison saw as "in there working for information that we didn't feel was needed," and for which other safer sources existed.[97]

Morrison, accompanied by Sheck, Miller, [   ] and Apollony, spent much of these early morning hours moving to the various NSA elements trying to coordinate information. From the Command Center, the group went to B1 [   ] B3 [   ] [   ] and to the A8 CSOC [   ] organizations. Angered by the long walks from one area to another, Morrison later recalled the scene:

> I saw our separate enclaves, perhaps at their worst. In this incident we had to come to grips quickly with [   ] information flowing into several centers, separated by what seemed to me in the early morning hours, enormous distances.[98]

The need for a centralized current operations and crisis-management center – the concept of a single focal point for current Sigint operations – had surfaced in NSA's experiences during numerous crises in the 1960s: Cuba (1962), Cyprus (1964), the Middle East (1967), Korea/*Pueblo* (1968), and Czechoslovakia (1968). This latest crisis provided another compelling reason for establishing a national crisis center. It became a major priority for NSA officials in the months ahead. The establishment of a "National Sigint Operations Center" (NSOC), diligently pursued by Morrison, was given its final push by his frustration in dealing with the shootdown of the EC-121.

Morrison's entourage reached the CSOC area about 0330 hours, or 0830Z, almost four hours after the shootdown. By this time, Spencer had compiled the [   ] tracking information and was ready to issue a NSA Follow-Up to the [   ] CRITIC. Morrison, however, wanted a coordinated A Group/B Group report, including Soviet, KORCOM, and [   ] tracking data. He held up the report awaiting B Group analysts to deal with the Korean [   ] tracking information. This activity, [   ] personnel arrived in the CSOC area, lasted until shortly after 0500 hours.[99]

OGA

EO 1.4.(c)
P.L. 86-36

BODY-32

Lieutenant General Marshall S. Carter, Director, NSA, June 1965 – July 1969

As officials at NSA attempted to sort out the crisis in the early hours of that April morning, action continued in the Far East. At 0625Z, [____] issued a SPOT Report declaring a Sigint Readiness ALFA at that site based on the possible shootdown.[100] The issuance of this SPOT report[101] was a formal acknowledgment of the critical situation. The Sigint Readiness ALFA was a standby situation designed to keep concerned elements alert during indefinite periods of tension. Certain changes in intercept, processing, and reporting techniques were required. USN-39 and USN-39P, a Navy Sigint detachment located at [_____] also declared Sigint Readiness ALFA. The latter based its alert on possible Soviet reaction to the shootdown – specifically, Soviet reconnaissance flight activity over the Sea of Japan.[102]

At the same time [_____] Chief B1105, who had been called into the B Watch Office, contacted the [_____] when informed of the ALFA declaration by [_____] Initially, questioning the ALFA as perhaps being a bit "premature," [____] asked whether any [____] warnings had been sent [_____] [_____] an analyst at [_____] relayed the information on the three advisory warnings and receipts at Fuchu. but surmised that it was most likely that the aircraft had received the [_____] [_____] had hit the deck, and thus was below [_____] radar coverage. He also informed [____] of the [_____] This communication took place at 0715Z, two and a half-hours after the shootdown. Before this [_____] conversation ended, Morrison and Apollony, who were still in the B Watch Office, agreed to the [____] ALFA. By this time, the additional information from the North Korean press release had come in. Morrison agreed, in response to a query from General Charles H. Bonesteel III (Commander of U.S. and UN Forces in Korea), that [_____] This information was to be passed to James R. Harris, the senior official [_____] With key Washington officials now aware of the incident through the [____] CRITIC, pressure was on the Agency to provide more information on the shootdown. The [____] [_____] in the Pentagon, for example, in constant touch with the Command Center and CSOC, requested additional information.[104] Evidence was mounting that the plane had indeed been a victim of North Korean aggression. With the plane long overdue at Osan, the North Korean English-language press release of the shootdown made it highly unlikely that the plane had "hit the deck" and escaped the attack. At 0935Z, General Carter established Sigint Readiness BRAVO HANGAR for NSA and all addressees because of the "possible shootdown." This action upgraded the previously declared ALFA [_____] and USN-39P and called for immediate reporting by the field stations as information became available.[105] The BRAVO alert, usually called for by NSA headquarters, required maximum response and a high degree of watchfulness for further developments in a serious situation. Although the BRAVO alert was supported by B Group, the message drafted by Apollony of B05 and [_____] Chief, A8, encouraged the maintenance of the lower ALFA alert for the A Group Sigint sites.[106] Based on the fact that the Soviets had exhibited no hostile tendencies, ALFA status was established for USA-30 (Wakkanai, Japan), USN-39, and USA-38.

With the establishment of the BRAVO HANGAR alert, the shootdown now attained a "crisis" status that had not been possible from field site reports. The first of many BRAVO HANGAR reports came at 1234Z.[107] This was the combined A and B Group effort that Morrison had insisted upon in the CSOC area earlier that morning. This report emphasized the [_____] 0435-0504Z period. It showed the KORCOM fighter aircraft from Hoemun intercepting the mission aircraft and reflected them returning to base. The unusual appearance of the Fishbed MIG-21s was also noted. In addition, the report listed the advisory warnings sent

P.L. 86-36

EO 1.4.(c)
EO 1.4.(d)
P.L. 86-36

OGA

EO 1.4.(c)
P.L. 86-36

out by [ ] and the Radio Pyongyang announcement of the shootdown. Although Soviet air and sea activity in the area of the shootdown was also noted, the report concluded that there was no direct evidence of Soviet involvement in the shootdown.[108] The most controversial part of the report was one line which stated that the closest approach made by the mission flight to the North Korean coast was [ ] with coordinates listed as [ ] It was at first assumed that the latter coordinate was [ ] which placed the aircraft only [ ] off the Korean coast.[109] A change to this report was soon sent by NSA correcting the second coordinate to [ ]

OGA

In midmorning of the shootdown day, [ ] Executive Assistant to the Director, received a call from the Central Intelligence Agency informing him that Richard M. Helms, Director of CIA, had instructed the Sigint Committee (which included NSA) to immediately look into the shootdown, including the requirements for the flight, tasking, personnel, and the classified materials on board. Helms wanted a preliminary report by the end of the following day (16 April) and a "complete" report within a week. [ ] immediately requested that field sites send all pertinent information to NSA headquarters.

P.L. 86-36

Despite unofficial reports that the North Koreans had shot down the plane apparently well beyond their declared air and water space of 12 miles, the Nixon administration decided to take a low-key approach to the crisis. House Minority Leader, Gerald R. Ford, explained that more than the "fragmentary info" then available was needed for a full evaluation. The Pentagon press release included the fact that the plane was flying a track that kept it at least 50 miles from the North Korean coast. In contrast, during the English-language statement issued from Pyongyang, the North Koreans accused the United States of a deep intrusion into their territorial air. In order to avoid the controversy that had arisen over the location of the *Pueblo* during the previous year, the Nixon administration wanted a careful reconstruction of the incident to refute the North Korean claims.

EO 1.4.(c)
P.L. 86-36

Accordingly, during the early hours of 15 April, A and B Group personnel at NSA carefully plotted the tracking information [ ] [ ] of the EC-121 and the reacting MIG fighters. The Joint Chiefs of Staff, the Defense Department, and the U.S. delegation to the United Nations all pressed NSA during the following days to analyze this information and provide proof that would definitely refute the claims of the North Korean government. To provide this information, NSA analysts conducted detailed studies to determine the closest approach that the EC-121 made to the North Korean coast and its exact location when it was shot down.

The first official NSA statement on the proximity of the aircraft to the North Korean landmass was the one which contained the confusing incomplete coordinates. [ ] [ ] This report concluded that the closest approach, as determined [ ] at that

EO 1.4.(c)
P.L. 86-36

time, was [____] and occurred at 0423Z.[112] The lengthy Recon Reaction Report, also produced by B Group and issued on the evening of 15 April, contained very detailed tracking information[____]

[____] This report noted the closest approach, [____] as [____] at 0300Z. It also concluded that the mission aircraft was [____] from North Korean territory and [____] from Soviet territory when initially reflected as merged with the MIG aircraft at 0444Z (41-23N, 131-35E).[113] The [____] figure also appeared in the second BRAVO HANGAR Report, issued a few hours later, which also placed the shootdown at approximately 90 nm from the North Korean coast at 41-10N, 131-40E.[114]

In the effort to provide the most complete and accurate data on the tracking information, NSA officials looked to other sources to confirm their findings. On 16 April, B11 requested [____] to forward all tracking information [____] between 0200-0530Z on 15 April[____] NSA used this information to issue a Change #1 to BRAVO HANGAR Report #2. This new [____] [____] indicated that the plane may have approached as close as [____] to the Korean landmass between 0304-0309Z. The report, however, noted that during the same time period [____] reflected the aircraft 80–90 nm from the North Korean coast.[116]

EO 1.4.(c)
EO 1.4.(d)
P.L. 86-36

Another item reporting a possible [____] approach by the aircraft caused additional consternation at the White House Situation Room because of its terminology. Issued by JSPC, it used the terms "tenuous evidence" and "questionable" reflections to report the location.[____]

White House officials wanted to know the reason for the use of these terms. NSA responded by stating that the trackings did not always reveal the true flight path of an aircraft.[117]

NSA's role in providing accurate tracking information was further enhanced following a White House meeting of representatives of the Department of State, Department of Defense, the CIA, and Joint Chiefs of Staff. Unsure of the accuracy of the tracking data and the probability of error in calculating it, the Joint Chiefs tasked NSA with describing the exact manner in which it calculated the aircraft's positions at all times and the possible margins of error in these calculations.[118] This material was requested by 18 April. On that day President Nixon was to hold a press conference.

The question of the closest approach of the U.S. aircraft[____] [____] was also of major concern to the U.S. delegation to the United Nations. The Nixon administration wanted to go before the Security Council on this incident, and it wanted to be very sure about the position of the EC-121 and any possible inconsistencies in its location.[119]

The NSA response to these position and tracking questions was the issuance of BRAVO HANGAR Report #7 early on 18 April. This reported the [____] tracking by [____] [____] radars during two critical portions of the mission – first during the closest approach of the aircraft to the North Korean landmass – and second during the KORCOM reaction and shootdown period.[____]

EO 1.4.(c)
P.L. 86-36

OGA

NSA's response was vital in providing the Nixon administration proof that the U.S. reconnaissance plane was over international waters when attacked.

EO 1.4. (c)
P.L. 86-36

THE INTELLIGENCE COMMUNITY ON THE DEFENSIVE

In the days following the shootdown, other segments of the intelligence community, namely DIA and JCS, also called upon NSA to help provide detailed answers regarding the shootdown. Facing Congressional hearings, these agencies expected hostile questions relating to whether the intelligence stake was worth the risk to U.S. ships, planes, and men. The *Washington Post* of 17 April reflected this feeling, ending its editorial with a reference to these peripheral flights as "arm's length electronic spying" that was unconventional and dangerous.[122] Senator J. William Fulbright of Arkansas, Chairman of the Foreign Relations Committee, stated that there was no type of information that he could conceive of that warranted the risks being taken. "That," said the *New York Times*, "was one of two immediate questions raised by the downing of the plane. The other dealt with the need for better protection, assuming the flights were deemed necessary."[123]

Reacting to such questions, DIA, which appeared to be unprepared to deal with them on its own, turned to NSA on 17 April to help provide detailed answers for General Joseph F. Carroll, DIA Director, who expected to testify before the Special House Subcommittee hearings on the *Pueblo* and EC-121 incidents on the following day. Carroll anticipated hard questions dealing specifically with the intelligence value of the peripheral flights off the [   ] coasts. He wanted to know what unique information the flights collected and what would be the intelligence loss if they were terminated. Carroll's request also asked for specific examples of collection successes in that area and specific examples of what intelligence the EC-121 collected. General Carroll wanted this information by 0700 hours on the following day.[124] In its response NSA officials emphasized the need for airborne coverage [   ] in peripheral areas.

[   ] While upholding the general need for reconnaissance flights, NSA officials took a harsh view of the Navy VQ-1 flights. They described the Comint "take" of the VQ-1 missions as primarily tactical in nature and processed at USN-39.[125]

On 18 April, NSA received a similar request from the Joint Chiefs of Staff. This request suggested that NSA and DIA collaborate in the preparation of a briefing back-up

32

book for the Chairman of the Joint Chiefs of Staff, General Earle G. Wheeler. Wheeler also expected to testify before the House Armed Services Subcommittee, and like Carroll, expected hostile questions. The JCS put forth three specific concerns: (1) the need for the number of flights currently taking place in the shootdown area (in anticipation of criticism that no protection was provided); (2) the [   ] for the flights; and (3) the value and use of intelligence of previous flights over the same area.[126] NSA quickly provided responses to the first and third items. While upholding the value of the airborne collectors, the response clearly differentiated between the Air Force ACRP platforms as compared to the Navy fleet support collectors, a point that had been only hinted at in the response to General Carroll. In a short memorandum that accompanied the NSA response, Morrison emphasized this point, stating that, from NSA's viewpoint, the superiority of the USAF platforms as Comint collectors was a prime consideration in determining the overall effectiveness of the program. [   ]

[   ] Morrison stated that based on information available, Comint collection by the VQ-1 (EC-121) missions was minimal compared with other collectors and generally duplicated by other sources. Morrison went on to cite the value of the VQ-1 flights for Elint collection of North Korean radar systems in the eastern half of the country. However, he emphasized that the Comint collection on the flights was primarily for advisory warning purposes. Overall, Morrison vigorously defended the need for the ACRP platforms, but was reticent in regards to the Navy VQ-1 flights. If there had to be cutbacks in the number of reconnaissance flights, Morrison preferred it to be in the Navy program.[127]

Morrison's downgrading of the value of the VQ-1 flights raised a major controversy with DIA officials. NSA and DIA disagreed over the value of the Navy flights at a Sunday, 20 April meeting of representatives of the two agencies (which included Morrison). Morrison noted in a memorandum the following day that NSA felt free to express its viewpoint unilaterally to the Joint Staff. This caused a strong reaction from the "Command Section" of DIA, especially from [   ] expressed to Morrison his strong disapproval of the NSA action in a phone conversation on 21 April. [   ] believed that NSA was providing information over and above that requested. Morrison countered by stating that NSA wanted to stress the importance of retaining the Air Force ACRP fleet in case the JCS was confronted with a query (by Congress or otherwise) regarding the impact of reducing airborne collection operations. When Morrison argued that input from the VQ-1 flights to NSA had been minimal for the past year and a half, [   ] questioned how NSA could fairly evaluate VQ-1 collection.[128]

Following this exchange, Morrison ordered K Group (with input from A, B, G, and P2) to prepare a study on the value of VQ-1 and VQ-2 reconnaissance activities covering the past two years. Morrison knew that senior analysts and reporters in A Group and B Group had previously assessed the VQ-1 intelligence as of minimal value. It was, according to them, duplicative of intelligence obtained from ground sites and other airborne collection. However, Morrison admitted that part of the problem could be the failure of the Navy to pass adequate information to NSA. He had recently been made privy to several excellent "Electronic Warfare" reports issued by VQ-1 on four EC-121 missions made before the shootdown. Morrison wished to have these reports examined closely for unique intelligence.[129]

A further study by B Group upheld the original assessment of the value of the VQ-1 flights as minimal [   ] According to the new study, during the past two years only [   ] tapes containing KORCOM air activity had been forwarded by VQ-1. The tapes, of only fair to poor quality, yielded unique information in

OGA

OGA

OGA

EO 1.4.(c)
P.L. 86-36

33

only one instance (and this was not used to produce intelligence). None had been passed to USM-81 (Yong-Dong Po) in two years. However, [⬛⬛⬛⬛⬛⬛] a small amount of nonduplicative material was passed on the naval and air problems but none contributed to product reporting.[130] A B Group message to NSAPAC on 23 April put it more bluntly, "There would be no Comint loss if the current level of VQ–1 flight scheduling was reduced to zero!"[131]

EO 1.4.(c)
P.L. 86-36

DEFENDING THE SIGINT RESPONSE TIME [⬛⬛⬛⬛⬛⬛]

In addition to providing detailed tracking information on the shootdown and arguing the value of the reconnaissance program with other parts of the intelligence community, NSA also played a major role in defending the Sigint response [⬛⬛⬛⬛⬛⬛] to the shootdown emergency.

General Wheeler called upon NSA to help explain the reason for the time delay in notifying Washington of the shootdown. The *Washington Post* on 17 April raised this "time delay" by questioning the "intolerable communications gap" that lasted nearly an hour. The newspaper compared the delay with the maximum 30-minute warning the United States expected to have in a missile attack.[132] Wheeler also asked NSA to provide convincing evidence that the president could be contacted quickly in emergency situations.

To deal with these time-delay questions, B05 developed a chronology of events. It asked overseas sites to provide a detailed chronology of actions taken pertinent to the shootdown – calls made, OPSCOMM exchanges, tip-offs issued, and the gists of texts.[133] This was being done, B05 emphasized, not to assign blame for any lapses but to aid the Sigint community in better performing its role in the future.[134]

Following the responses, NSA produced a 46-page composite chronology of the event. The period of time covered in the chronology was from the departure of the EC-121 from Atsugi Naval Air Station at 14 April 2159Z until 16 April 1730Z 1969. The most important references used to compile the chronology were the NSA-produced Final Recon Reaction Report (15-2344Z) and Supplements, NSA Sigint Readiness BRAVO HANGAR Report Seven (18-0558Z) and the chronologies of USN-39 (Kamiseya), USA-58 (Hakata), USF-790 (JSPC) [⬛⬛⬛⬛⬛⬛].

It was [⬛⬛⬛] of course, that played the most critical role during the shootdown period with its tracking of KORCOM radar, its advisory warning role, and its eventual issuance of a CRITIC. Therefore, the defense of the Sigint community by NSA was largely a defense of the actions carried out by [⬛⬛⬛] on that April afternoon.

OGA

The NSA report stressed the Sigint station's first responsibility as its advisory warning role – to issue warnings of hostile intent that enabled the mission aircraft to take evasive action in time. Based on the enemy tracking information, NSA concluded that [⬛⬛⬛] had sent the warnings as soon as possible. The initial detection of the [⬛⬛⬛] fighter track occurred at 0436Z, and the [⬛⬛⬛⬛⬛⬛] followed two minutes later, after the validity [⬛⬛⬛] was confirmed, at 0438Z. By 0440Z, when the fighters were determined to be within 50 nm of the aircraft, [⬛⬛⬛] sent the first [⬛⬛⬛⬛⬛⬛]. A SPOT report of the fighter reaction was issued at 0445Z and a second [⬛⬛⬛⬛⬛] at 0448Z.

While examining the [⬛⬛⬛] role, NSA officials initially had to deal with some incorrect information passed by CINCPAC in a 15 April message. CINCPAC reported that the EC-121 flight had actually acknowledged the advisory warnings issued by [⬛⬛⬛] This information was relayed by DIRNSA and used in early reporting to the White House. NSA queried the Fifth Air Force about the source of the information. NSA officials believed that Navy aircraft were not equipped with the [⬛⬛⬛] equipment and were

P.L. 86-36

prohibited from acknowledging any [____] broadcasts. NSA officials later learned that the acknowledgment transmissions were from the ground operator at Fuchu prior to his broadcasting them to the aircraft by the [____] format.[135] Unfortunately, the "misinformation" was reported to the President's Intelligence Board as well as to President Nixon himself. Asked for his opinion on the cause of this mistake, [____] [____] Executive Assistant to the Director, NSA, replied that he knew of no specific cause of the error. However, he cited the lack of a centralized authority for Elint collection as a major part of the problem. The President's Board had expressed this very need for a centralized and definitive Elint authority several years before when it examined NSCID No. 6.[136] Despite this weakness NSA believed that the Sigint community, specifically [____] performed its duties well in accordance with the [____] directive. According to the NSA report, [____] correctly followed all procedures, passing the warnings to the broadcast station at Fuchu, which was not under NSA control. At that point, the Sigint role in the warning system ended.

OGA

NSA officials also examined [____] role in making Sigint information available to operational commanders who could use it to initiate actions, such as the scrambling of fighters. NSA officials emphasized in their report that during the critical shootdown period (0438 to 0546Z) [____] reported that information was forwarded in real-time to the Fifth ADVON via KY-3 secure voice circuits and to the 314th Air Division Warning Center via OPSCOMM to permit operational actions to be taken by the commanders concerned. In addition, the station also reported that tapes of [____] reports were sent by OPSCOMM to USA-58 for relay to the Fifth Air Force.[137] While the [____] chronology included the OPSCOMM exchanges with the 314th Air Division, including several tip-offs of KORCOM fighters being reflected by North Korean radar, no exact logs of these exchanges were kept by either [____] or the Fifth ADVON.[138] However, Colonel [____] [____] Chief, JSPC, declared that there appeared to have been no failure on the part of the Sigint system to properly warn operational forces in this incident.[139]

EO 1.4.(c)
P.L. 86-36

NSA also investigated [____] issuance of a CRITIC in the shootdown. Several days after the incident, the National Military Command Center (NMCC) in the Pentagon asked NSA if the time lapse between the apparent time of shootdown (0447Z) and the time of the initial CRITIC (0544Z), nearly an hour, was considered normal.[140] Morrison and Carl Miller, the Deputy Chief of B11, gave the National Military Command Center and Secretary of Defense Melvin R. Laird and his deputy, David Packard, a briefing on the subject. Miller, in the first part of the briefing, stressed NSA's belief that the Soviet tracking was more reliable than the North Korean. Morrison then described the chain of events at [____] He emphasized the time that the field site had spent in analyzing the available information, checking with other stations, and determining whether or not the plane had entered the Japanese Air Defense Identification Zone (ADIZ). While explaining the reasons for the time delay between the shootdown and the CRITIC, Morrison emphasized that he believed that the station had conducted itself in a highly creditable manner.[141]

NSA officials also saw the need to explain the CRITIC system to military commanders who apparently did not fully understand its purpose. The Fifth Air Force, for example, especially questioned the timeliness of the CRITIC issue. NSA responded that the CRITIC was not a vehicle for providing initial alerts to operational commanders. The CRITIC report in question provided no substantive information that had not been previously dealt with in SPOT reports or conveyed more rapidly by voice and OPSCOMM channels. From the standpoint of the commands, NSA concluded, their initial concerns about the delivery time of the CRITIC were unfounded. The real purpose of the CRITIC was to inform Washington level authorities of extraordinary intelligence.[142]

EO 1.4.(c)
P.L. 86-36

~~TOP SECRET UMBRA~~

Several days later, as Carter prepared for a personal appearance before a closed session of the House Appropriations Committee, Morrison was still examining the role of [redacted] He tasked K1 with looking into the [redacted] that were issued on Sea of Japan flights during the past 90 days. He also demanded details on the one [redacted] that was recently issued. Morrison was especially concerned with specified procedures that could be taken by reconnaissance flights to reduce the likelihood of KORCOM radar detection and interception. Were these maneuvers intuitive actions of the individual pilot? Were they performed in the past to avoid continuing radar tracking? Morrison believed that the answers to these questions would provide more evidence that the judgment of [redacted] was impeccable in its issuance of a CRITIC.[143]

B Group prepared its response to Morrison. It cited COMSEVENTHFLT Operation Order 307 which called for planes to avoid provocative or hostile maneuvers and to "turn away from" Sino-Soviet or other unfriendly territory. While a [redacted] under this order did not require the aircraft to divert its course, a [redacted] called for it to take a course "directly away from" the North Korean or Chinese coastline and prepare for defense against hostile attacks. These "preparations for defense" were not actually spelled out in the order. However, the B Group response pointed out that in the case of the slow, cumbersome EC-121, it would seem logical that the pilot would elect to hit the deck and rely on low altitude and maximum available speed for protection. Unlike the faster EA-3Bs assigned to VQ-1, the EC-121s were not equipped with an internal DECM (Defensive Electronic Counter-Measures) system which could jam enemy radar.[144] An observation of the evasive maneuver, however, would most likely be a very rare occurrence. Since the beginning of 1969, USA-58 had issued [redacted] [redacted] all to USAF [redacted] flights equipped with the [redacted] system. [redacted] to a [redacted] (PACAF high-altitude photography mission) in March via the Fuchu station. The B Group report concluded that the belief that the mission might have "dropped to the deck" was a valid hypothesis based on sound tactical concepts.[145]

Central to the entire CRITIC question was how quickly the president was informed in an emergency situation. The JCS again asked NSA officials to supply convincing evidence that the president could be contacted quickly. It was to include examples of 10 incidents with a brief narrative on each, in which NSA provided such information to the president. The request stated that Secretary of Defense Laird desired to make a statement that "all national level officials receive information on these emergency situations within 10 minutes."[146] NSA responded to this request by giving an account of the CRITIC reporting system. The system, as operated by NSA and the Service Cryptologic Agencies (SCA), required information meeting the CRITIC criteria to reach Washington customers no later than 10 minutes after such information was recognized as critical. Recipients were to receipt for any CRITIC within two minutes. NSA listed 12 1968–69 incidents in which CRITICS were issued. [redacted]

[redacted] In the EC-121 incident, the NSA officials reported that a CRITIC was released two minutes after the shootdown was determined to be probable (0542Z). It met CRITIC requirements since it was receipted for by Washington customers within seven minutes of its 0544Z release time.[148] NSA's defense seemed to satisfy Congress. The Congressional subcommittee's final report of this incident concluded that the CRITIC was received in the White House Situation Room at 0550Z, six minutes after being issued by [redacted] and one hour and three minutes after the estimated time of shootdown. However, Congress still wanted to know when the president had been notified.[149] Henry A.

OGA

Kissinger, Assistant to the President for National Security Affairs, reported that he notified Nixon by phone at about 0400 hours (approximately four hours after the shootdown) that the facts were being put together. Kissinger again called the president at 0700 hours to arrange a meeting with him in the Oval Office later that morning, with initial reports by the State and Defense Departments then available.[150]

On 23 April, General Carter forwarded a copy of NSA's report to the JCS Chairman, General Wheeler, with the assessment that "the system does work and works quite well." This conclusion by the NSA Director strongly supported the belief put forth in the Morrison-Miller briefing that [ ] performed commendably in sending out warnings to the aircraft, informing the military commands, and issuing a CRITIC only after careful examination of all available data revealed that the plane was probably a victim of hostile actions.

THE NIXON ADMINISTRATION'S RESPONSE TO THE SHOOTDOWN

The shootdown of the EC-121 was the first major foreign crisis faced by President Richard M. Nixon. He had repeatedly used the *Pueblo* incident in his fall election campaign to state the need for new leadership. He stressed that there would be no "*Pueblo*" during his administration, no incident in which a "fourth-rate" power would show total disrespect for the United States. While a Congressional investigation into the previous year's *Pueblo* incident was continuing, the new Nixon administration was forced to deal with the shootdown crisis. It dominated newspaper headlines for several days and remained a major news story for several weeks.[151]

The press described the Washington reaction to the EC-121 incident as a "cautious" one, with Nixon maintaining a "deliberate calm."[152] Secretary of State William P. Rogers reflected this cautious response in his address to newspaper editors on 16 April when he said "the weak can be rash; the powerful must be more restrained."[153] President Nixon made no public statement on the shootdown until a press conference on 18 April.

EO 1.4.(c)
P.L. 86-36

Using information provided by NSA, Nixon answered a number of questions about the shootdown at his press conference. He also revealed that he had ordered the resumption of reconnaissance flights and vowed to provide protection for the unarmed planes. Although he did not announce it at the press conference, the president also instructed the U.S. Navy to assemble a task force of aircraft carriers, destroyers, and perhaps a battleship to rendezvous south of the Sea of Japan.[154] In defending his administration's actions and the reconnaissance flight Nixon declared that in contrast to the *Pueblo* incident, there was no doubt as to the plane's whereabouts before and during the shootdown. Nixon said that the United States knew what the Soviet and North Korean radars reflected that day. He enhanced the account to include American radar as showing the exact same thing. Nixon said that this information totally refuted the North Korean claim that the EC-121 violated its airspace. Nixon's public statement concerning North Korean and Soviet radar reflections caused a major reaction at NSA. The Deputy Director, Louis Tordella, was greatly concerned over the release of such sensitive information and its possible impact on future Sigint successes.[155] [ ]

[156] In a related action, [ ]

EO 1.4.(c)
EO 1.4.(d)
P.L. 86-36

as possible.[157] Despite Tordella's concern no drastic changes occurred as normal reporting of North Korean and Soviet radar reflections continued in the BRAVO HANGAR reports.

President Nixon and Henry Kissinger favored
strong retaliatory measures against North Korea.

In addition to assembling a task force and the call for the resumption of reconnaissance flights, the Nixon administration also responded unfavorably to the North Korean request for another meeting of the Military Armistice Commission meeting at Panmunjom. The United States simply delayed its reply; administration officials felt that another meeting would be a propaganda vehicle for the North Koreans and that a walkout by its delegation would probably occur before an American response. The JCS advised the UN Command under General Bonesteel on 16 April to refrain from a response until further advice from Washington arrived.[158] At that time the MAC meeting was one of several options being considered by Nixon and his advisors. Another was to take the matter directly to the United Nations Security Council. This course, however, was looked upon as a probable cause of embarrassment to the Soviet Union which would most likely have to come to the defense of its ally before this public forum.[159]

After several days, Nixon administration officials made the decision to keep the channels of communication with North Korea open. U.S. officials called for a 290th meeting of the Military Armistice Commission on the morning of 18 April. The opening North Korean statement, made by Major General Yi Choon-sun, the senior North Korean representative, made no mention of reconnaissance flights but accused the UN Command of many ground violations along the DMZ. Major General James B. Knapp, the senior U.S. member of the delegation, responded, accusing the North Koreans of an "unprovoked attack" upon an aircraft that was making a routine reconnaissance flight similar to many flown since 1950. Using the NSA intelligence information then available, Knapp stated that at no time did the aircraft penetrate or closely approach the 12-mile airspace claimed

EO 1.4.(c)
P.L. 86-36

by North Korea. Attributing the necessity of these flights to repeated acts and threats of aggression by the North Koreans, he further defended the right of these "legitimate reconnaissance operations" to take place as long as they remained outside of territorial waters. Knapp stated that the North Koreans must have, in some respect, shared this view since they found it necessary to fabricate an account of violated airspace. He concluded with the remark that this was not an isolated incident but only another in a long list of violations of international law.[160] Following his prepared address, General Knapp led a walkout of his delegation after the North Koreans refused to respond. As the Americans departed from the room, General Yi demanded to know what was the "belonging" of the plane, a remark that raised much subsequent debate among U.S. and South Korean government officials and political observers.[161] No one ever fully understood the North Korean response.

One option considered by Kissinger's White House staff as a response to the shootdown was to seize some North Korean ships at sea. A rumor arose that a Korean-owned ship under Dutch registry was somewhere in transit to North Korea. Nixon wanted to seize that ship. NSA became involved in a frantic search for the vessel. Based on a presumed departure date of 28 March from the Netherlands, the vessel should have been in the vicinity of Cape Town, South Africa. The ship was never found; Kissinger questioned if in fact it ever existed.[163]

As the National Security Council discussed possible administration responses to the North Koreans, Rogers and Laird favored a moderate approach while Kissinger and President Nixon favored strong retaliatory measures. Task Force 71, that Nixon had ordered into the Sea of Japan, was a compromise measure, and with its 250 available war planes, left open a possibility for retaliation.

The task force, which was not mentioned in Nixon's press conference of 18 April and not reported in the press until the following day, was activated by CINCPAC, Admiral John S. McCain, Jr., at 0324Z on 16 April. The deployment included three attack carrier strike groups under the nuclear powered USS *Enterprise* (CVAN-65), the USS *Ticonderoga* (CVA-14), and USS *Ranger* (CVA-61); an antisubmarine carrier support group under the USS *Hornet* (CVS-12); an air defense group under the guided missile cruiser USS *Chicago* that also included the four vessels that participated in the search and recovery operations, USS *Sterett*, USS *Dale*, USS *Mahan*, and USS *Tucker*; and a surface action group that included the cruisers USS *Oklahoma City* and USS *St.Paul*.[165]

On that same day, 16 April, the Commander of the Seventh Fleet, Vice Admiral William P. Bringle, issued a call for Sigint support. The most urgent request was for technical support

As originally conceived by the U.S. policymakers, the task force left open the possibility that Washington would respond with military force to the shootdown. As defined by CINCPACFLT, the main objective of Task Force 71 was to prepare to conduct strike operations in the Sea of Japan when directed by higher authority. Initial attack

39

goals would be to neutralize the air order of battle of North Korea, gain air superiority, strike selected airfields, and destroy maximum enemy aircraft on the ground. U.S. policymakers did not expect Soviet and CHICOM forces to intervene.[167] The only response to the assembling of the task force was that Soviet naval units continuously shadowed the major U.S. ships and Soviet Badger aircraft reconnoitered the task force. There was also a mild diplomatic rebuke by Soviet Ambassador Dobrynin to the Department of State. He urged the Americans to act with "reasonableness and restraint" in connection with the Korean incident, stressing that the Soviets could not help but look cautiously upon the large American force off its coast. The Department of State countered that the Soviets were in a position to moderate tensions through contacts with North Korea, the perpetrator of the incident.[168] By 26 April Task Force 71 began to depart from the Sea of Japan. On that day, the JCS directed CINCPAC to redeploy most of the task force to normal Seventh Fleet operations in Southeast Asia. By 1 May only the destroyers USS *Sterrett* and USS *Rowan* remained off the east coast of Korea, having been directed to assume duties as seaborne ground intercept (GCI) platforms.[169]

The press stressed the role of Task Force 71 as part of the president's order to resume, with protection, the reconnaissance flights over the Sea of Japan. However, as the result of a general stand-down of peripheral reconnaissance flights, the only opportunity that the task force had for protecting the ACRP flights came on 24 April. A special ☐☐☐☐ flight over the Sea of Japan, the first since the shootdown, was carried out with no hostile reaction from the North Koreans.[170]

The Defense Department initiated this stand-down of reconnaissance activity on 15 April. The Commander of the Seventh Fleet, Vice Admiral Bringle, ordered VQ-1 to cancel all reconnaissance flights along the ☐☐☐☐☐ periphery until further notice and Admiral John S. McCain, Jr., CINCPAC, authorized only USAFSS ☐☐☐☐☐ flights over the South Korean landmass, south of the 37th parallel. He canceled all flights ☐☐☐☐☐☐☐☐☐☐ Two BEGGAR SHADOW and two ☐☐☐☐☐☐ missions were also canceled soon after these orders were given. NSA officials concerned with intelligence coverage ☐☐☐☐☐ responded by calling for full 24-hour coverage ☐☐☐☐☐ by those ☐☐☐☐☐ flights still allowed while the restrictions were in force.[171] The stand-down of reconnaissance flights over the North Pacific continued for nearly three weeks. Despite President Nixon's order, the JCS delayed implementation while they studied methods of protection. Nixon was unhappy with this JCS delay.[172]

OGA

☐☐

By 21 April, U.S. intelligence was convinced that North Korean responses were strictly defensive in nature. A watch panel meeting of U.S. Forces, Korea, held on that date concluded that there was considerable evidence of general alert posture and overall

EO 1.4.(c)
P.L. 86-36

increased readiness for defensive purposes, rather than for hostile action against the United Nations Command in South Korea.

A DIA memorandum of 23 April, which detailed North Korean military reactions following the EC-121 and *Pueblo* incidents, put forth similar views. DIA reported that the readiness posture assumed by the North Koreans appeared to be primarily defensive in nature, with no indications that the country was preparing for offensive operations. As in the *Pueblo* action, the KORCOM reactions were taken in anticipation of possible U.S. retaliatory actions. The series of aircraft deployments, including the MIG 15/17 fighters from Hoemun, was taken, the DIA report concluded, probably because of the U.S. Navy Task Force operations off the North Korean coast. As in the *Pueblo* incident of the year before, there were no significant North Korean Navy operations other than some ships being warned to be on antiaircraft alert.[175]

FORMAL REVIEWS AND RECOMMENDATIONS

A special subcommittee of the House Committee on Armed Services was meeting to investigate the January 1968 capture of the USS *Pueblo* and the internment of its crew members when the shootdown occurred. The subcommittee was chaired by Otis G. Pike (Democrat – New York). L. Mendel Rivers (Democrat – South Carolina) headed the full Armed Services Committee. He argued for a strong retaliation against the North Koreans following the EC-121 shootdown. Rivers added the investigation of the EC-121 shootdown to Pike's subcommittee.

Asked to testify before the House subcommittee on the EC-121 incident were General Earle G. Wheeler, Chairman of the Joint Chiefs of Staff, and Brigadier General Ralph D. Steakley, United States Air Force _____ of the Joint Chiefs of Staff.   OGA
Their testimony on the EC-121 took place on 25 April, ten days after the shootdown. Steakley initiated a number of contacts with NSA on the morning of 15 April to prepare for his testimony. Both he and General Wheeler, as has been seen, received copies of the NSA-compiled chronologies of the shootdown period. Wheeler also received the NSA and DIA responses to questions relating to the need of the reconnaissance program and the value and use of intelligence produced by it, as part of a briefing back-up book used at the hearings.[176]

In response to the testimony of Wheeler and Steakley, the subcommittee acknowledged that the reconnaissance activity was necessary to ensure the availability of information essential to national security interests. The subcommittee, however, was not convinced that the magnitude of the reconnaissance activity, and the many millions of dollars spent to support NSA and DIA activities, was completely justified. The subcommittee, therefore, recommended that the full Armed Services Committee monitor more closely the operating activities of both of those agencies.[177]

The protection of the flights was another major concern of the subcommittee. At the time of the hearings, only one overwater [   ] mission had been flown since the EC-121 shootdown and it was supported by Task Force 71. Wheeler told the subcommittee that an evaluation process was continuing to determine the best way to provide future protection to reconnaissance flights, not only over the Sea of Japan, but all high risk areas. Representative Lucien N. Nedzi (Democrat – Michigan) questioned why this had not been done following the 1965 incident involving the North Koreans. Wheeler's response was that flights had indeed been escorted after that incident, but because of the expense and no further reaction from the North Koreans, it had been discontinued. For several days after the *Pueblo* incident, Wheeler continued, this escort was revived. A combat air patrol creating a protective plane barrier between the reconnaissance aircraft and the land mass from which hostile aircraft might come was in effect until July 1968. At the time of the EC-121 the policy for air reconnaissance missions off the coast of North Korea was a [   ] with a strip alert from the South Korean mainland for contingency protection. General Steakley further testified that since 1965 there had been only one instance of a Korean fighter coming close to a U.S. reconnaissance aircraft.[178] The subcommittee then attempted to determine if DIA, who had the responsibility of evaluating risk on these flights, participated in the decision to no longer require fighter escort on the flights. Further testimony revealed that the decision appeared to have been made solely by the Joint Chiefs of Staff and the Department of State; DIA was merely informed of the change in plans.[179]

The most critical findings of the subcommittee related to command control responsibilities.[180] Citing the failure of the operating command of the EC-121, VQ-1, of being included on warning messages to the aircraft, the subcommittee concluded that serious deficiencies existed in the organizational and administrative command structures of both the Navy and the Department of Defense.[181] According to the subcommittee, the EC-121 incident again strikingly illustrated, as in the *Pueblo* incident, the inability of the system to relay information in a timely and comprehensible fashion to those charged with the responsibility for making decisions. According to Chairman Pike, the unacceptable delay in initiating search and rescue efforts was due to the apparent fragmentation of command responsibility and authority of the military units involved. The subcommittee recommended that the Joint Chiefs of Staff review the entire military reconnaissance program with an emphasis on establishing clear and unmistakable lines of command control.[182]

The command control aspect of the EC-121 incident was also examined by two official executive office study groups in the weeks following the shootdown. One was a CINCPAC Board of Evaluation, the second a JCS Ad Hoc Fact Finding Group. Admiral John S. McCain, Jr., CINCPAC, directed the establishment of the board. It was to look into all aspects of the EC-121 shootdown. The board, under Rear Admiral John N. Shaffer, made an investigative field trip to several sites in the Japan-Korea area in late April and early May 1969. These included the Fifth Air Command and PACOM Elint Center (PEC) at Fuchu, the Naval Security Group at Kamiseya, VQ-1 at Atsugi,[   ] and the 314th Air Division at Osan, Korea. NSA participation in the Shaffer board study included an appearance before the board by Admiral Lester R. Schulz, Chief of NSAPAC. Admiral Schulz repeated the NSA position that the Sigint role in the crisis, especially [   ] in its warnings to Fuchu and coordinating with and informing Fifth ADVON/314th Air Division,[   ] USA-58, was proper and correct. He also upheld [   ] on the time of its CRITIC issuance. His recommendations included a review of PARPRO scheduling to eliminate marginally productive flights and to ensure full tasking on those

OGA

EO 1.4.(c)
P.L. 86-36

42

carried out. Schulz also outlined the need for preflight information being made available to appropriate direct service activities to aid in more accurate and timely reporting.[183]

While the CINCPAC study focused on the command control aspect of the EC-121 shootdown, the JCS formed its Fact Finding Group to also examine the command control structure. On 5 May, it designated Major General K.B. Reaves as the senior member of a JCS four-member informal ad hoc fact-finding body. Major emphasis was to be on the reaction times of military commands involved in the incident. To avoid unnecessary duplication of effort, the JCS group drew upon the report of the CINCPAC Board. The JCS also authorized direct liaison with NSA for support.[184] General Morrison and Carl Miller repeated their earlier Pentagon briefing for this group on 1 May.

The consensus of these studies was the need to improve command and control communications in general. Both groups concluded that protection for reconnaissance flights into sensitive areas required more coordination between the Sigint community and Air Force operational commands with the protective responsibility. A specific recommendation called for integrating Sigint information with operational information at command and control centers where decisions could be made based on all-source information. Several proposals were considered and by September 1969 a Fifth Air Force/PACAF concept for a Command Advisory Function (CAF) system emerged.

Awaiting approval from the JCS of the CAF concept, CINCPAC decided to implement immediately the hardware portion of the plan. This called for the installation of Special Intelligence (SI) secure OPSCOMM circuits between Sigint intercept sites and the CAFs as well as circuits between CAFs. CINCPAC called upon Schulz (NSAPAC) to serve as a focal point for coordinating and implementing new circuits from SCA locations to the CAFs.[185]

During the installation of the hardware between the CAFs and the Sigint units, PACAF Operation Plans (OPLANS) for PARPRO missions were also put into effect. Protection of these missions was dependent upon early warning radar information and fighters on strip alerts as available from (a) a U.S. Navy GCI picket ship in the Sea of Japan off the Korean coast; (b) Task Force 71 forces remaining in the Yellow Sea; and (c) strip alert fighters at Misawa, Japan, and various bases in South Korea, Okinawa, and Taiwan. The Air Force also activated Command Advisory Functions while these plans were being implemented. The CAFs activated to serve the Korean-Japanese area were the 314th Air Division/Fifth ADVON CAF, Osan Air Base, from which fighters had been sent following the EC-121 shootdown, and the Fifth AF CAF at Fuchu Air Station, Japan. These CAFs were located at the lowest echelon of command that had the need for Special Intelligence information and the authority to employ or direct forces. They served as focal points capable of assimilating and correlating on a near real-time basis all-source information affecting operations in the PACOM geographical area. This information was to keep the USAF commander apprised of the current situation in his area of responsibility. It included receiving and acting upon information pertaining to PARPRO missions, and if required, directing protective actions.

A Naval Board of Inquiry into the loss of its EC-121 provided a further look at the shootdown incident. Admiral Bringle, the Seventh Fleet Commander, ordered this board

EO 1.4.(c)
EO 1.4.(d)
P.L. 86-36

43

EO 1.4.(c)
P.L. 86-36

convened on 20 April 1969 at the U.S. Naval Station, Atsugi, Japan. The board met from 24 April to 6 May 1969 and came up with two major recommendations. One was for a careful assessment of the [____] warning procedures under the [____] [____] The second was for procurement of higher performance aircraft to replace the EC-121 aircraft.[187] The EC-121, with its low maximum speed and altitude limitations was viewed as vulnerable in peripheral hostile areas. For the remainder of 1969, the number of VQ-1 flights in the [____] area was severely cut back. The EC-121s were used only in the lower-risk [____] Pacific area. By the 1970s the EC-121s were phased out, replaced in the VQ squadrons by Lockheed EP-3E Orion turbo-engined aircraft with higher speed and altitude capabilities.[188]

The most important question that arose from the Naval Board of Inquiry was related to the [____] Following the CINCPAC recommendations relating to improving the Navy's participation in the [____] the Navy Board recommended the installation of the [____] data link communications equipment in all reconnaissance aircraft. The faster time factor and the automatic receipt (by equipment aboard the aircraft) feature made it preferable to the [____] (DO NOT ANSWER) warning method. In the case of the EC-121 it would have at least eliminated the uncertainty about whether the aircraft received the three warning messages [____] [____] The Navy Board considered the [____] installation a long-term action. On an interim basis it recommended an immediate broadcast of [____] warning message by the Sigint site through a direct patch provided by the broadcast station. This eliminated an encode/decode/encode process. It also provided an instantaneous warning broadcast capability for command control. The JCS approved this plan and directed its implementation on 1 March 1970.[189]

While the shootdown spurred the Navy to recommend the phaseout of the EC-121, the heavy loss of life also sparked community-wide interest in the use of unmanned collection platforms. The development of these unmanned platforms, or drones, came out of the CINCPAC study group. In late May, General Morrison asked P04 to look into the possibility of a collection drone flying one of the [____] tracks.[190] P04 found that the possibility of using drones in a reconnaissance role had already been investigated. Lieutenant Colonel Andrew Corra, in charge of unmanned reconnaissance systems on the Pentagon's Air Staff, was in San Diego consulting with the Ryan Aeronautical Company when he saw a newspaper headline on the EC-121 shootdown. He decided to initiate an alternative way of carrying out Elint missions, a way which eliminated risking human life. Corra flew back to Washington and approached General Steakley of the [____] of the JCS about his drone idea. Steakley said that he would pursue the matter with Cyrus R. Vance, Deputy Secretary of Defense. Within a month after the EC-121 shootdown, the Defense Department approved the program using the Ryan model TE drone aircraft. The first test flight took place in November 1969 and the first operational flight occurred on 15 February 1970 [____] [____]

This unmanned drone operation was given the nickname [____] and was part of an Air Force program initially referred to as the [____] [____] The Air Force soon adopted the use of drones and "minimanned" aircraft (flight crews only) with palletized intercept receivers remotely tuned by operators at ground stations to reduce manned aerial reconnaissance in high risk areas. Through a complex system of uplink/downlink communications, intercept activities could be carried out without exposing a large number of operator personnel to hostile reactions. These drone and minimanned platforms supplemented the ACRP fleet. However, because of cost considerations and a high attrition rate due to the drones over North Vietnam, the Air Force phased out the [____] drone operation in 1975. Nevertheless, a downlink

OGA

program[_____]continued[_____]in the late 1970s, using minimanned U-2R aircraft. Two U-2R aircraft performed a total of 24 missions per month[

]

EO 1.4.(c)
P.L. 86-36

A FINAL LOOK AT THE CRISIS

Despite minimal official involvement in BEGGAR SHADOW missions, NSA played a major role in evaluating the shootdown of EC-121. It provided accurate information on the flight pattern of the mission[_____]radar reflections of the flight; and command and control responsibilities. In the investigation which followed the crisis, NSA officials provided key intelligence information justifying the aerial reconnaissance program and the need for this special intelligence and made important recommendations for improving the U.S. response to crisis situations. Ironically, the loss of 31 lives and the practice of double-loading flights for training or liberty purposes never really surfaced as a major concern. To be sure, some officials such as General Morrison pointed out that such practices were contrary to normal operating procedures and should never have been established on a long, dangerous mission or on a "lumbering EC-121 aircraft," but the issue was never addressed in the major postincident investigations. The Naval Board of Inquiry report, for example, dealt only with describing the crew as "properly trained and briefed, and necessary for the aircraft mission." Only the low speed aircraft itself was described as limited for employment in peripheral, potentially hostile areas.

In light of the hostile nature of the North Korean regime in the late 1960s, the *Pueblo* incident, and the continuation of very threatening language by the Kim regime, the sending of a large crew on a slow-moving plane to hover off the North Korean coast for many hours reflected extremely questionable judgment on the part of U.S. policymakers. The NSA message of 23 December 1967 to the JCS/JRC, prior to the deployment of the USS *Pueblo*, cited various incidents involving the North Koreans that reflected the very hostile nature of that regime. This campaign of hostility continued throughout 1968 as evidenced by the Blue House raid, the *Pueblo* seizure, and the massive campaign of subversion and sabotage on the east coast of South Korea by 120 North Korean commandos late in that year. Although NSA itself did not send out a warning message prior to the EC-121 shootdown, there was the COMUSKOREA message addressed to CINCPAC just four days before which conveyed the unusually vehement and vicious language by the North Koreans in warning UN forces of provocative actions. CINCPAC passed this information to VQ-1 and[_____]which included a suggestion for crews to be especially alert and to be prepared to abort the mission. Seventh Fleet (which carried out a final review of this mission on 14 April) and CINCPAC, however, did not regard the threat as serious enough to cancel these flights. General Wheeler, in the Congressional hearings, cited the 190 flights that had taken place (without incident) over the Sea of Japan in the early months of 1969 and the lack of serious reactions against U.S. reconnaissance aircraft by the North Koreans since the 1965 incident as justification for CINCPAC reaction. However, in light of these North Korean threats, perhaps more consideration should have been given to curtailing some of these sensitive missions, particularly those of lesser intelligence value.

After the shootdown, the JCS severely restricted reconnaissance flights off the[_____]
[_____]coasts. VQ-1 cut back its missions[_____]and used only the faster, higher altitude EA-3Bs for the remainder of 1969. It is interesting to note that

DOCID: 4047116

in May 1971 (two years after the shootdown) CINCPAC reacted to the presence of MIG-21s at the Hoemun Air School (the exact situation that existed just prior to the April 1969 shootdown) by placing the flights beyond the range of the North Korean GCI capability.[193] In 1969 the situation aroused only speculation by NSA's JSPC facility as to the significance of MIG-21s at Hoemun. In 1971 experience caused a more prudent policy of flight restrictions.

Vice Admiral Noel Gayler,
Director of NSA, Aug 1969 – July 1972

The shootdown caused the entire collection program to be reevaluated. It brought U.S. military reconnaissance operations again under serious public scrutiny. The press, the U.S. Congress, and various investigative boards all questioned whether the value of these flights equaled the risks involved. For NSA, the shootdown presented the challenge of defending an entire collection program over a reconnaissance flight of questionable value. Just four days after the shootdown, the JCS ordered a review of all data obtained from the airborne collection platforms. The JCS request put pressure on NSA to justify the need for a massive reconnaissance program. During the rest of 1969, NSA participated with the JCS/JRC, DIA, and the military commands in the reconnaissance review. K18 was the focal point of the study at NSA. It collected precise data on each mission and evaluated the uniqueness of the data each mission produced (compared with ground sites). In December 1969 NSA concluded this thorough review by upholding the need for the reconnaissance program.[194]

NSA's thorough examination of aerial reconnaissance activity encouraged greater Navy cooperation with NSA. Admiral Bringle, Commander, Seventh Fleet, committed a number of EC-121 sorties for primary tasking by NSA. The new NSA Director, Admiral Noel Gayler, met with Bringle and Admiral John H. Hyland, CINCPACFLT, while on a Far East and Southeast Asian trip in November 1969. Both appeared willing to improve the Navy's former policy of permitting only limited NSA tasking. However, they still qualified their cooperation by stating that "only if it did not interfere with fleet support requirements." Hyland was unwilling to commit a fixed number of sorties per month for NSA tasking. Gayler viewed the Navy acceptance of more NSA tasking as a partial success.[195] By early 1970, the Navy did make a greater number of VQ-1 flights available for "National" tasking, with 10 flown in March and 14 more proposed for April of that year.[196]

In addition to effecting a thorough review of the aerial reconnaissance programs, the EC-121 shootdown acted as a catalyst in promoting a more comprehensive NSA role in monitoring PARPRO activity. Under Morrison's direction, K1 prepared and initiated a program at NSA to more thoroughly evaluate the intelligence "take" from the various

46

mission tracks. K18 created an evaluation branch of five personnel to work in coordination with representatives from A, B, G, P2, and P04.[197] Morrison also encouraged greater participation by NSA in the [____] Reconnaissance Review meetings attended by JCS/JRC, DIA, and NSA representatives. The JCS/JRC conducted these meetings during the latter part of [____] to prepare the reconnaissance schedule for the following month. In obvious reaction to the EC-121 shootdown, Morrison suggested that NSA representatives pay closer attention to Elint schedules that were primarily a DIA responsibility. Although NSA was tasked with only a technical collection assessment on the Elint flights, Morrison called for NSA representatives to keep very precise, accurate logs of these meetings to provide documentation of the positions, judgments, conclusions, and recommendations of all agencies involved.[198] Eugene Sheck recalled that the NSA review of the JCS/JRC [____] had been rather passive, almost lackadaisical, before April 1969. After the EC-121 incident, NSA's role changed to that of a serious monitor of the reconnaissance flights. After the shootdown, DIRNSA took the program more seriously, never missing or postponing the [____] briefing sessions that took place.[199]

Perhaps the most lasting result of NSA's review of the shootdown was the renewed push for, and eventual establishment of, the National Sigint Operations Center (NSOC). The EC-121 crisis was the "last straw," in the words of Morrison, in showing the deficiencies in the fragmented approach to Sigint operations at that time.[200] According to Morrison, a central analytical capability was necessary to examine and evaluate multisource data.

The renewed effort to establish a Sigint center began shortly after the EC-121 shootdown. That long April morning when General Morrison had been called by the existing Command Center to personally direct the situation convinced him to push for the creation of such a center. Outgoing NSA Director Carter concurred in the establishment of what he referred to as a National Sigint Operations Center. He recommended combining the various communications and personnel resources represented by the existing Command Center and the A8 and B Watches. Carter asked Morrison to develop a plan for the proposed center, the communications required to serve it, and the manpower necessary to operate it on a 24-hour a day, 7-days a week basis.[201] On 25 July 1969 Morrison tasked the P2 organization to develop a detailed plan for the new center. He proposed that the center be thought of in terms of a Sigint Support Center – providing service to NSA's worldwide Sigint customers as well as to the national cryptologic system.

A September 1969 concept paper gave the broad outlines of the present-day NSOC. However, planning for the Sigint center was slowed by a number of problems including the identification of a suitable location and opposition to the idea within NSA itself. Almost three years would pass before the concept would be finally implemented.

In February 1972 Morrison, still the ADP, directed that planning to relocate the A Watch (CSOC) accommodate an NSOC. On 4 May 1972, Dr. Louis W. Tordella, Deputy Director, requested Morrison to submit his current views on the proposed NSOC. General Morrison gave a quick response on 5 May. He saw CSOC becoming the first component of the NSOC when it moved to its new quarters. The NSA Command Center and other representative elements would be phased in over a period of 10 months. The OPSCOMM circuits would be pulled together in the same area.[202]

On 11 July 1972 Morrison appointed a task force under Charles R. Lord to implement the establishment of the NSOC. By December of that year NSOC had achieved an initial, although limited, operational capability with sufficient OPSCOMM equipment to facilitate activation of nearly 45 circuits. NSOC was formally inaugurated on 21 February 1973 with a ribbon-cutting ceremony. It became fully operational by the fall of that year, in time to deal with the Arab-Israeli Yom Kippur War of October 1973.

OGA

The concept of a single focal point for current Sigint operations came from the crises of the 1960s, especially the EC-121 shootdown. With the establishment of NSOC, NSA became an even more important source in providing, in General Carter's words, the "whole story" to Washington when other organizations were unable to react knowledgeably to the situation.[203] The chronology of the shootdown compiled by NSA was vital in upholding the Sigint community role in the crisis and instrumental in the Morrison-Miller Pentagon briefings. Related to this was NSA's aid in helping the military commands to better integrate Sigint intelligence into their own command and control network. Finally, NSA clearly defined the CRITIC system to the military commands and reaffirmed that the White House could indeed be notified quickly of an emergency situation. As Morrison stated, "The system worked, and it worked extremely well," but he saw the need for it to work even better. Thus the establishment of NSOC.[204]

The National Sigint Operations Center was the result of Morrison's expressed need to improve the overall system. NSOC represented a unique capability. Today it functions as the only organization devoted to time-sensitive information in a total national intelligence system. Among its many functions are monitoring all collection systems and activities of the United States Sigint system, providing guidance to field stations, optimizing Sigint collection in anticipation of high-interest situations, maintaining a close watch over time-sensitive Sigint reporting, and reviewing and releasing time-sensitive Sigint product. Finally, as envisioned by General Morrison during the 1969 EC-121 situation, NSOC serves as a crisis management center for NSA and the entire United States Sigint system, acting as executive agent and overall coordinator of CRITIC reporting.[205]

NOTES

1. Tai Sung An, *North Korea in Transition* (Westport, Connecticut: Greenwood Press, 1983), p. 133. Hereafter An.

2. "Behind North Korea's Belligerence," *Time*, April 25, 1969, p. 24.

3. [_____] "The National Sigint Operations Center," *Cryptologic Spectrum* (Summer 1979) 9:10. (S-CCO) Hereafter [_____]

4. Conversation, Lieutenant General Marshall S. Carter and Major General John E. Morrison, Jr., 25 August 1970, Oral History Files, NSA Historical Collection, NSA. (TSC) Hereafter Carter-Morrison Conversation.

5. [_____] p. 4.

6. Robert A. Divine, *Since 1945: Politics and Diplomacy in Recent American History* (New York: Alfred A. Knopf, 1979), p. 14. Hereafter Divine.

7. John Lewis Gaddis, *Russia, the Soviet Union, and the United States: An Interpretive History* (New York: John Wiley and Sons, Inc., 1978), p. 200. Hereafter Gaddis.

8. Divine, p. 30.

9. Joseph C. Goulden, *Korea: The Untold Story of the War* (New York: Times Books, 1982), p. 30.

10. Ibid., p. 37; M. T. Haggard, "North Korea's Foreign Policy: The Meaning of the *Pueblo* and EC-121 Incidents," Library of Congress Legislative Reference Service (June 18, 1969), F-384:11. Hereafter Haggard.

11. Joungwon Alexander Kim, *Divided Korea: The Politics of Development, 1945–1972* (Cambridge: Harvard University Press, 1975), pp. 182-83.

12. Gaddis, p. 201.

13. Ibid., p. 249.

14. Divine, p. 183.

15. An, pp. 131–33, and Philip Shabecoff, "The Problems of a 'Porous War'," *New York Times*, April 27, 1969. Hereafter Shabecoff.

16. Shabecoff.

17. Richard Halloran, "North Korean Pressure on U.S. Dates to Kim's 66 War Cry," *Washington Post*, April 17, 1969, p. A9.

18. Haggard, p. 11.

19. Tae-Hwan Kwak, ed., *U.S.-Korean Relations 1882–1982* (Kyungnan University: Institute for Far Eastern Studies, 1982), p. 268.

20. An, p. 170.

21. Haggard, pp. 7–8; NFOIO, message to CINCPACFLT, 161650Z April 1969. (TSC); and "Orders of Battle Pertinent to North Korean Shootdown," *DIA Intelligence Supplement*, 17 April 1969, Series VIII Crisis Files, #27, NSA Historical Collection, NSA. (TSC-NF) (Hereafter, all Sigint source documents are found at this location unless otherwise specified.)

22. U.S. Congress, House of Representatives, Committee on Armed Services, *Inquiry into the USS PUEBLO and EC-121 Incidents*, Hearings Before the Special Subcommittee on the USS *PUEBLO*, 91st Congress, 1st Session, 1969, p. 818. Hereafter Congress, Inquiry..

23. A.D. Horne, "North Korea, U.S. Meet on Plane," *Washington Post*, April 18, 1969, p. A10.

24. [_____] *A Special Historical Study of the Airborne Communications Reconnaissance Program 1961–1964* (San Antonio: United States Air Force Security Service, 1965), p.20. (TSC) A copy of this is located in Series X.J.1.2, NSA Historical Collection, NSA.

25. Ibid., p. 8. (TSC)

26. Ibid., pp. 56–60. (TSC)

27. DIRNSA, memorandum to Secretary of Defense, "Sigint Airborne Communications Reconnaissance Program," 13 November 1964. (TS) Series VI.CC.1.1, NSA Historical Collection, NSA.

28. [_____] Special Historical Study, p. 26. (TSC)

29. Ibid.

30. Jeffrey Richelson, *The U.S. Intelligence Community* (Cambridge: Ballinger Publishing Co., 1985), p. 267. The United States Intelligence Board was formed in 1958. It is chaired by the Director of Central Intelligence and includes the Directors of the National Reconnaissance Office (NRO), NSA, and the Bureau of Intelligence and Research (INR) of the Department of State. Other members include representatives from the FBI, Departments of Energy and Treasury, and the Deputy Director of the CIA. The Assistant Chiefs of Staff for Intelligence of each military service sit as observers.

31. United States Intelligence Board, memorandum for USIB Principles, "Mission Basis for Downed EC-121M Navy Aircraft," 18 April 1969. (TS-CCO)

32. Interview, Eugene Sheck, 23 July 1987, by Robert D. Farley and [_____] OH 20-87, NSA Oral History Collection, NSA. (TSC) Hereafter Sheck Interview, OH-20-87.

P.L. 86-36

49

TOP SECRET UMBRA

BODY-54

33. DIRNSA, message to USN-39, 10227Z March 1969. (SC)

34. Sheck Interview, OH 20-87. (TSC)

35. NSA (P), "Background Material on EC-121 Incident," 16 April 1969. (TSC) This report was prepared for the use of Major General John E. Morrison, ADP, for his Pentagon briefings. (TSC)

36. Commander in Chief Pacific Fleet (CINCPACFLT), message to Commander in Chief Pacific (CINCPAC), 161026Z April 1969. (TS)

37. NSA, memorandum, "Review of Bonnie Blue and Headstrong Procedures," undated. (TSC) Hereafter Memo: Bonnie Blue.

38. NSA, memorandum, "VQ-1 Elint Collection by EC-121 Aircraft Flying Track 5H8263 During 1969," undated. (S)

39. Arthur Levenson   (TS)

40. SSO Strategic Air Command (SAC), message.   (S-CCO)

41. Memo: (SC)

42. NSA (P), memorandum.   (SC)

43. Dick Van der Aart, *Aerial Espionage* (New York: Arco/Prentice Hall Press, 1985), p. 59. Hereafter Van der Aart.

44. DIRNSA, message to   (SC)

45. U.S. Congress, *Inquiry into the USS Pueblo and EC-121 Incidents*, p. 818.

46. Commander U.S. Forces Korea (COMUSKOREA),

(S)

47. *7th Fleet Inquiry*, Lewis Testimony. (S)

48.

49. National Military Command Center, memorandum for the record, "Missing U.S. Navy EC-121 Aircraft," 151125Z April 1969. (TS)

50. NSA, Sigint Summary   (TSC)

51. USF-790, message to Oscar Two/Golf Bravo distribution, 301100Z March 1969. (SC)

52. Hereafter, times in this study will be given in Greenwich Mean, or Zulu Time. To determine the local time in the Far East, add nine hours. For Eastern Standard Time, subtract five hours.

53. NSA (P), "Background Material," Tab Eleven, Sigint Equipment List. (S-CCO)

54. Office of the Secretary of Defense, "*Pueblo* Review Paper, EC-121 Excerpt," 13 November 1969, pp. 25–26. (TSC)

55. NSA (P04), memorandum, "Roles of   and USN-39 in Crisis," undated. (SC)

56. OSD, "*Pueblo* Review Paper," pp. 26–28. (TSC)

57. NSA (P04), "Roles of USA-38 and USN-39." (SC)

58. USN-39, message, 171625Z April 1969. (SC)

59. The complete trackings of the EC-121 and the North Korean fighters is detailed in NSA, "Final Recon Reaction Report," 2/0   R16-69, 152344Z April 1969; Supplement 1, 170012Z April 1969; and Supplement 2, 180305Z April 1969. (TSC)

60.   message, 171500Z April 1969. (SC)

61. USN-39, message, 171625Z April 1969. (SC)

62. NSA, Comint Report, 2/0   /R07-69, Sigint Readiness BRAVO HANGAR Report Number Seven, 180558Z April 1969. (SC)

63.   message, 171500Z April 1969. (SC)

64.   message, 171500Z and USA-58, message, 162026Z April 1969. (SC)

OGA

65. USA-31, message, 171500Z April 1969. (SC)
66. Office of the Secretary of Defense, memorandum, "*Pueblo* Review Paper – EC-121 Excerpt," 13 November 1969. (TS)
67. USAFSS, message, 161439Z April 1969. (SC)
68. [redacted] Executive Assistant to Director, memorandum to Executive Secretary, President's Foreign Intelligence Advisory Board. "BEGGAR SHADOW Advisory Warning," 22 April 1969. (TS)
69. NSAPAC OFFICE [redacted] message to DIRNSA [redacted] 148, 220554Z April 1969. (SC)
70. [redacted] Spot Report, 2 [redacted] R73-69, 150445Z April 1969. (SC)
71. *7th Fleet Inquiry*, Testimony of [redacted] Commanding Officer, VQ-1. (S)
72. [redacted]
73. *7th Fleet Inquiry*, Testimony of [redacted] C.O., USNSG, [redacted] p. 24. (S)
74. USA-58, message, 162026Z April 1969. (TSC)
75. USAFSS, message, 161439Z April 1969. (SC)
76. USA-31, SPOT Report Follow-Up No. 2 to 2/H6/KCK/R373-69, 150520Z April 1969. (SC)
77. [redacted] message, 171500Z April 1969. (SC)
78. [redacted] CRITIC 1-69 to DIRNSA, 150544Z April 1969. (SC)
79. Ibid.
80. Foreign Broadcast Information Service, Bulletin No. 11, 150717Z April 1969. Copy in Series VIII, Crisis 27, NSA Historical Collection, NSA.
81. Foreign Broadcast Information Service, Bulletin No. 15, 150807Z April 1969. Copy in Series VIII, Crisis 27, NSA Historical Collection, NSA.
82. JRC Q/A, "Re: Time Elapsed Before Dispatch of Interceptor Aircraft to Shootdown Area."
83. JRC Q/A, "Re: Time Elapsed Between Shootdown and Launch of Search and Rescue Operations."
84. CTU 70.2.3 (VQ-1), message, 260937Z April 1969. (TS-CCO)
85. Ambassador James D. Beam, despatch to Secretary of State, William P. Rogers, 151146Z April 1969. (U).
86. William P. Rogers, despatch to [redacted] 151915Z April 1969. (S)
87. National Military Command Center, memorandum, "Missing USN EC-121 Aircraft," 161155Z April 1969. (TS)
88. Rogers, despatch to [redacted] 171619Z April 1969. (C)
89. National Military Command Center, memorandum, "EC-121 SAR Operations," 191742Z April 1969. (S)
90. USNAVINVSERVRA SASEBO, message, 200700Z April 1969. (S)
91. FAIRECONRON ONE, message to DIA, 181531Z April 1969. (TS)
92. Naval Scientific and Tech Group, Far East (NSTFE), Report, [redacted] (C)
93. Interview [redacted] 29 October 1987, by Robert D. Farley and [redacted] OH 28-87, NSA Oral History Collection, NSA. (S-CCO) Hereafter [redacted] Interview, OH-28-87.
94. Ibid.
95. NSA Command Center [redacted] (TSC)
96. Sheck Interview [redacted] (TSC)
97. Interview Major General John E. Morrison, Jr., and Carl A. Miller by Robert D. Farley and [redacted]
98. Major General John E. Morrison, Jr., memorandum, "National Sigint Ops Center (NSOC)," 5 May 1972. (S)
99. [redacted] Interview, OH 28-87. (S-CCO)
100. [redacted] Spot Report, 2 [redacted] /R377-69, "Declaration of Sigint Readiness Alfa," 150625Z April 1969. (SC)
101. This can be issued by NSA Headquarters or a Sigint element with a reporting mission.
102. [redacted] Spot Report, 2 [redacted] /R1233-69, 150739Z April 1969. (SC)
103. Telecons between NSA B Watch Office [redacted] and NSAPAC Representative [redacted] 150710-0745Z April 1969. (TS)
104. [redacted] Interview, OH 28-87. (S-CCO)
105. DIRNSA, message, P21-046, 150935Z April 1969. (SC)
106. [redacted] Interview, OH 28-87. (S-CCO)
107. This is the first of 52 reports issued until the termination of the alert on 30 April.
108. NSA, Comint Report, 2/0 [redacted] /R-03-69, Sigint Readiness BRAVO HANGAR Report No. 1, 151234Z April 1969. (SC)
109. NSA Command Center, "Records of Event Log," 0700-1530 EST 15 April 1969. (TSC)
110. [redacted] Executive Assistant to DIRNSA, memorandum, "Sigint Meeting on EC-121 Shootdown," 15 April 1969. (S)
111. NSA, Final Recon Reaction Report, 152344Z April 1969. (TSC)

P.L. 86-36

P.L. 86-36

OGA

EO 1.4.(c)
P.L. 86-36

P.L. 86-36

P.L. 86-36

P.L. 86-36
P.L. 86-36

EO 1.4.(c)
P.L. 86-36

P.L. 86-36

P.L. 86-36

EO 1.4.(c)
P.L. 86-36

112. NSA, Comint Report, 2/0☐/R03-69, Sigint Readiness BRAVO HANGAR Report No. 1, 151234Z. (SC)
113. NSA, Comint Report, 2/0☐/R16-69, Final Recon Reaction Report No. 355-69, 152344Z April 1969. (TSC)
114. NSA, Comint Report, 2/0☐/R04-69, Sigint Readiness BRAVO HANGAR Report No. 7, 160237Z April 1969. (SC)
115. DIRNSA, message, B11-419, 162049Z April 1969. (SC)
116. NSA, Comint Report, Change 1 to 2/0☐/R04-69, Sigint Readiness BRAVO HANGAR Report No. 2, 170220Z April 1969. (SC)
117. NSA (B051), Telecon to JSPC, 161447Z April 1969. (SC)
118. Assistant Secretary of Defense to Director, Joint Staff, JCS, memorandum, "Analysis of Evidence Concerning EC-121 Incident," 17 April 1969. (TS SENS)
119. SSO New York, message to DIRNSA☐ 171600Z April 1969. (TS CCO)
120. NSA (B11), Telecon to NOG, 152155Z May 1969. (SC)
121. NSA, Comint Report, 2/0☐/R07-69, Sigint Readiness BRAVO HANGAR Report No. 7, 180558Z April 1969. (SC)
122. Editorial, "The EC-121 Incident," *Washington Post*, April 17, 1969, p. A20.
123. Peter Grose, "Caution on Plane Urged in Capital," *New York Times*, April 16, 1969, p. 14.
124. DIA, memorandum to NSA (Madison Mitchell), "Request for Information for General Carroll," 17 April 1969. (SC)
125. NSA, draft of memorandum in Response to DIA Request for Information for General Carroll, 17 April 1969. (TSC)
126. JCS, memorandum to DIA and NSA, DJSM 576-69, "EC-121 Shootdown," 18 April 1969. (TS)
127. NSA, memorandum to Director, Joint Staff, N0375, "EC-121 Shootdown," 20 April 1969. (TS)
128. NSA, memorandum, "Conversation with ☐ at Approximately 0930 Hours Local," 21 April 1969. (TS CCO)
129. NSA, memorandum (ADP to K1), "VQ-1 and VQ-2 Sigint Collection Activities," 22 April 1969. (TS CCO)
130. NSA, memorandum (B04 to K1), B04/273/69, "VQ-1 Sigint Collection Activities, 1967-79," 12 May 1969. (TSC)
131. DIRNSA, message to HQ NSAPAC, ADP-220, 232146Z April 1969. (TS CCO)
132. George C. Wilson, "Hopes Dwindling for Plane Crew; Debris Is Found," *Washington Post*, April 17, 1969, p. A9.
133. DIRNSA, message, B05/11/69, 160615Z April 1969. (SC)
134. DIRNSA, message to USA-38, B-05 00618, 170220Z April 1969. (SC)
135. NSAPAC OFFICE JAPAN, message to HQ NSAPAC, F41-136, 180643Z April 1969. (SC)
136. NSA, memorandum, "Visit with ☐" 22 April 1969. (S CCO)
137. HQ NSAPAC OFFICE☐, message to DIRNSA☐-148, 220554Z April 1969. (SC)
138. NSAPAC REP☐ message to DIRNSA (B Group Watch Officer), 202044Z April 1969. (SC)
139. JSPC, message to☐ JSPC-CH/139-69, 220525Z April 1969. (S CCO)
140. NMCC, memorandum to DIRNSA, "Disparity in Reporting Times," 170230Z April 1969. (TS)
141. Morrison-Miller Interview, OH 04-88, (TSC) and NSA, memorandum, "Morrison-Miller Briefing – 18 April 1969," 23 April 1969. (TSC)
142. NSAPAC OFFICE JAPAN, message to DIRNSA, F41-148, 220554Z April 1969. (SC)
143. NSA, memorandum, (ADP to K1), "Requirement for Further Information in Connection with the BEGGAR SHADOW Shootdown," 26 April 1969. (SC)
144. Ibid.
145. NSA, memorandum (B Group to ADP), "Response to ADP Requirement for Further Information in Connection with the BEGGAR SHADOW Shootdown," 27 April 1969. (S/NF)
146. JCS, memorandum to NSA, J3M-752, "Contact with the President in an Emergency," 18 April 1969. (C)
147. NSA, memorandum to National Military Command Center, "Memorandum for the Director, National Security Agency," J3M - 752/69 dated 18 April 1969, 19 April 1969. (S CCO)
148. NSA (P2), memorandum to the National Military Command Center, "Information Requested by General Wheeler," 24 April 1969. (TSC)
149. U.S. Congress, *Inquiry into the USS* Pueblo *and EC-121 Plane Incidents*, pp. 1677–78.
150. Marvin and Bernard Kalb, *Kissinger* (Boston: Little, Brown and Company, 1974), p. 93.
151. Carroll Kilpatrick and A. D. Horne, "President Maintains a Deliberate Calm," *Washington Post*, April 16, 1969, p. A1.
152. Ibid.
153. Max Frankel, "U.S. to Emphasize Diplomatic Steps on Loss of Plane," *New York Times*, April 17, 1969, p. 14.
154. Henry Kissinger, *White House Years* (Boston: Little, Brown and Co., 1979), p. 318. Hereafter Kissinger.
155. Seymour M. Hersh, *The Price of Power: Kissinger in the Nixon White House* (New York: Summit Books, 1983), p. 74. Hersh states that a former NSA analyst described the Nixon radar revelations as creating near

P.L. 86-36

OGA

P.L. 86-36
P.L. 86-36
P.L. 86-36

pandemonium at NSA and considered the Nixon statement as comparable to "Black Tuesday" when NSA defectors William H. Martin and Vernon F. Mitchell appeared at a Moscow press conference. The interviews conducted by Farley and ▨ with NSA employees who participated in the analysis and reporting of the event, however, did not affirm that the Nixon statement was looked upon as such a catastrophic event at NSA.

156. NSA, memorandum (ADP to Chiefs A,B,C,P04), "Impact of Recent Disclosures on Future Sigint Successes," 21 April 1969. (TS-CCO)

157. DIRNSA, message, B11-440, 191553Z April 1969. (SC)

158. JCS, message to CINCUNC, 7978, 162303Z April 1969. (S)

159. Max Frankel, "U.S. to Emphasize Dipomatic Steps on Loss of Plane," *New York Times*, April 17, 1969, p. 14.

160. Statement of James B. Knapp at 290th Meeting of Military Armistice Commission, Panmunjom, 18 April 1969. Available in Series VIII, Crisis 27, NSA Historical Collection, NSA.

161. There was much speculation by Western and Japanese analysts on what was behind the North Korean attack. Some believed General Yi was trying to identify the EC-121 as being involved with U.S. forces in Korea. Others thought he was trying to determine Japanese involvement in the incident, since the plane staged from Atsugi, Japan. Much speculation was related to the Kim regime's reunification hopes. The North Koreans hoped to weaken American morale in order to influence it to withdraw from its South Korean commitments. Some saw it as a test to see how strongly the new Nixon administration would respond to North Korean aggression. Would it go beyond the Johnson response to the *Pueblo*? Some analysts saw the attack as a continuation of the series of hostilities aimed at South Korea and its morale. Others saw it as an attempt to weaken U.S.-Japanese ties. There were strong opposition groups in Japan opposed to the renewing of the U.S.-Japan Security Treaty and increasing sentiment for reversion of Okinawa (occupied since the end of World War II by the United States). A more divergent viewpoint centered on a recent change of leadership in North Korea. Choe Hyun had recently become Defense Minister, representing a hardline faction assuming more power in the North Korean government. Some obervers believed Choe may have ordered the attack as a macabre birthday present to his old friend, Kim Il-So'ng. A noticeable lack of follow-up propaganda was noted in the days after the shootdown, possibly showing disagreement about the incident among high North Korean government officials. Only Choe issued a major statement, on 17 April, hailing the "heroic act" of the 896th Unit of the Korean People's Army. Hersh, in *The Price of Power* claims that the former NSA analyst he interviewed claimed that NSA soon concluded from intelligence that the incident was a command-and-control error involving a single North Korean airplane. He claimed that there was no evidence that the North Korean government knew of the attack before it occurred. The participants in the Farley ▨ interviews disagreed with this viewpoint. Most, including General Morrison, believed that the North Korean government was responsible for the shootdown. None could recollect any intelligence at the time of the incident that suggested otherwise.

162. NSA (B Watch Office), message to ▨, 170200Z April 1969. (SC)

163. Kissinger, *White House Years*, p. 318.

164. ▨ message, 182000Z April 1969. (SC)

165. National Military Command Center, memorandum, "Redeployment of 7th Fleet Task Force 71," 181846Z April 1969. (TS)

166. HQ NSAPAC, message, 162215Z April 1969, (S-CCO) and DIRNAVSECGRUPAC, message, 162347Z April 1969. (TS-CCO)

167. CINCPACFLT, message, 170451Z April 1969. (TS)

168. William P. Rogers, despatch to ▨ 220110Z April 1969. (C)

169. National Military Command Center, Memorandum for the Record, "Task Force 71 Operations," 012245Z May 1969. (S)

170. National Military Command Center, memorandum, "Activity of U.S. Forces in Northeast Asia," 242120Z April 1969. (TSC)

171. DIRNSA, message ADP-205, 152110Z April 1969. (S)

172. Richard M. Nixon, *Memoirs of Richard Nixon* (New York: Grosset and Dunlap, 1978), p. 385.

173. NSA, Comint Report, 2/0/KCJ-E/R01-69, Sigint Readiness BRAVO HANGAR Report No. 18, 210205Z April 1969. (SC)

174. SSC ▨ message, "▨ Watch Panel Meeting of 21 April 1969," 210801Z April 1969. (TSC)

175. DIA, memorandum, "North Korean Military Reactions Following the EC-121 and *PUEBLO* Incidents," 23 April 1969. (TSC)

176. JCS, memorandum for Directors of Defense Intelligence Agency and National Security Agency, "EC-121 Shootdown," 18 April 1969. (TS)

177. U.S. Congress, *Hearings on the USS* Pueblo *and EC-121 Incidents*, p. 923.

178. Ibid.

179. U.S. Congress, *Report on USS* Pueblo *and EC-121 Incidents*, p. 1677.

180. (U) Unlike the *Pueblo*, the EC-121 was under the normal operational chain of command. The plane was under operational control of VQ-1 which in turn was subordinate to the Seventh Fleet, CINCPACFLT and CINCPAC.

181. U.S. Congress, *Report on USS* Pueblo *and EC-121 Incidents*, p. 1619.

182. Ibid., p. 1625.

183. HQ NSAPAC, message to DIRNSA, [   ], 300317Z April 1969. (S-CCO)

184. JCS, memorandum for Major General K. H. Reaves, USA, Vice-Director, Joint Staff, "Ad Hoc Fact Finding Body," 5 May 1969. (TS)

185. [   ] and John B. Eastman, eds., *The Joint Sobe Processing Center 1961-1971* (NSA/CSS: United States Cryptologic History - Special Series, 1974), pp. 21-24. (TSC).

186. Ibid., p. 24. (TSC)

187. *7th Fleet Inquiry*, p. 47.

188. Van der Aart, p. 55.

189. Chief, Joint Chiefs of Staff, message, 271938Z February 1970. (TS-CCO)

190. NSA, memorandum, (ADP to P04), "Drones," 29 May 1969. (S-CCO)

191. William Wagner, *Lightning Bugs and Other Reconnaissance Drones* (Fallbrook, California: Aero Publishers, Inc., 1982), pp. 167–68.

192. [   ], *A History of the USAFSS Airborne Sigint Reconnaissance Program (ASRP) 1950–1977* (San Antonio: United States Air Force Security Service, 1977), pp. 40–54. A copy is available in Series X.J.4, NSA Historical Collection, NSA. (TSC)

193. CINCPAC, message to JCS/JRC, 080040 May 1971. Accession Number 16541, Cryptologic Archival Holding Area, NSA Archives. (TS)

194. NSA K1, Annual Report Calendar Year 1969, Series VI E-5-30, NSA Historical Collection, NSA. (TSC)

195. DIRNSA, memorandum, "Far East and Southeast Asia Issues and Problems," 10 November 1969. (TS-CCO)

196. NSA (ADP), memorandum to D1, "Comments on Director's Far East Trip Report," 14 May 1970. (TSC)

197. NSA K1, Annual Report Calendar Year 1969, Series VI E-5-30, NSA Historical Collection, NSA. (TSC)

198. NSA (ADP), memorandum to Chief, K, "Monthly Review of Reconnaissance Schedule," 15 May 1969. (S)

199. Sheck Interview, OH 20-87. (TSC)

200. Morrison-Miller Interview, OH 04-88. (TSC)

201. DIRNSA, memorandum to ADP, "Establishment of the National Sigint Operations Center," 17 July 1969. (C)

202. NSA (ADP), memorandum to Deputy Director, "National Sigint Ops Center (NSOC)," 5 May 1969. (S-CCO)

203. Carter-Morrison Conversation. (TSC)

204. Morrison-Miller Interview, OH 04-88. (TSC)

205. [   ] (S-CCO)

1.4.(c)
P.L. 86-36

P.L. 86-36

Notes on Sources

Primary Sources

Archival Holdings

Crisis Files, Series VI, NSA Historical Collection, National Security Agency (NSA), Ft. Meade, Maryland.

Crisis Files, Series VIII, Number 27, The EC-121 Shootdown, NSA Historical Collection, NSA, Ft. Meade, Maryland.

D33 Files, A-70-380, Retired Records, NSA, Ft. Meade, Maryland.

D42 Files, A-72-294, Retired Records, NSA, Ft. Meade, Maryland.

EC-121 Files, Locations CBOH 34,35,52, NSA Cryptologic Archival Holding Area, NSA, Ft. Meade, Maryland.

P04 Files, A-70-232, Retired Records, NSA, Ft. Meade, Maryland.

Discussion

Major General John E. Morrison, Jr. with DIRNSA, Lieutenant General Marshall S. Carter, "Need for NSOC," 25 August 1970, NSA Historical Collection, NSA. (S)

Oral Histories

P.L. 86-36

OH 31-87, 15 December 1987, NSA Historical Collection, NSA. (SC)

OH 02-88, 28 January 1988, NSA Historical Collection, NSA. (SC)

OH 26-87, 22 September 1987, NSA Historical Collection, NSA. (S)

General John E. Morrison, Jr. and Carl A. Miller, OH 04-88, 23 February 1988, NSA Historical Collection, NSA. (TSC)

Eugene Sheck, OH 20-87, 23 July 1987, NSA Historical Collection, NSA. (TSC)

OH 28-87, 20 October 1987, NSA Historical Collection, NSA. (S-CCO)

Official Documents

OGA

Joint Chiefs of Staff   Questions and Answers Re: EC-121 Shootdown, 1969.

U.S. Congress, House of Representatives, Committee on Armed Services, *Hearings Before the Special Subcommittee on the USS* Pueblo – *Inquiry into the USS* Pueblo *and EC-121 Plane Incidents*, 91st Congress, First Session, 1969 (Washington, D.C.: Government Printing Office, 1969).

U.S. Congress, House of Representatives, Committee on Armed Services, *Report of the Special Subcommittee on the USS* Pueblo – *Inquiry into the USS* Pueblo *and EC-121 Plane Incidents*, 91st Congress, First Session, 1969 (Washington, D.C.: Government Printing Office, 1969).

U.S. Navy, – Commander of the Seventh Fleet Board of Investigation,

Memoirs and Autobiographies

Kissinger, Henry A. *White House Years* (Boston: Little, Brown and Company, 1979).

Nixon, Richard M. *RN: The Memoirs of Richard Nixon* (New York: Grossett and Dunlop, 1978).

EO 1.4.(c)
P.L. 86-36

Secondary Sources

P.L. 86-36

Cryptologic Histories

and John B. Eastman, (ed.). *The Joint Sobe Processing Center 1961– 1971* (Ft. Meade: NSACSS, United States Cryptologic History, Special Series, 1974). (TSC)

Special Historical Study of the Airborne Communications Reconnaissance Program Vol. II – USAFSS Program 1961-1964 (San Antonio: United States Air Force Security Service, 1965). (TSC)

History of the USAFSS Sigint Reconnaissance Program (ASRP) 1950-1977 (San Antonio: United States Air Force Security Service, 1977). (TSC)

Special Historical Study of Sigint Support to Air Operations in SEA 1965-1971 (San Antonio: United States Air Force Security Service, 1972). (TSC)

Books

An, Tai Sung. *North Korea in Transition* (Westport, Connecticut: Greenwood Press, 1983).

Divine, Robert A. *Since 1945: Politics and Diplomacy in Recent American History* (New York: Alfred A. Knopf, 1979).

Gaddis, John Lewis. *Russia, the Soviet Union and the United States* (New York: John Wiley and Sons, Inc., 1978).

Goulden, Joseph C. *Korea: The Untold Story of the War* (New York: Times Books, 1982).

Hearsh, Seymour M. *The Price of Power: Kissinger in the Nixon White House* (New York: Summit Books, 1983).

Kalb, Marvin and Bernard. *Kissinger* (Boston: Little, Brown and Company, 1974).

Kim, Joungwon Alexander. *Divided Korea: The Politics of Development, 1945-1972* (Cambridge, Massachusetts.: East Asian Research Center - Harvard University, 1975).

Koh, Byung Chul. *The Foreign Policy of North Korea* (New York: Frederick A. Praeger, 1969).

Kwak, Tae-Hwan. ed. *U.S.-Korean Relations: 1882-1982* (Seoul: The Institute for Far Eastern Studies - Kyungnam University, 1982).

Richelson, Jeffrey. *The U.S. Intelligence Community* (Cambridge, Massachusetts: Ballinger Publishing Company, 1985).

Sullivan, John and Roberta Foss, eds. *Two Koreas – One Future* (Lanham, Maryland: University Press of America, 1987).

Van der Aart, Dick. *Aerial Espionage* (New York: Arco/Prentice Hall Press, 1986).

Wagner, William. *Lightning Bugs and Other Reconnaissance Drones* (Fallbrook, California: Aero Publishers, Inc., 1982).

Articles

"An Exercise in Restraint," *Newsweek* 73 (April 28, 1969): 27-31.

Burnham, James. "The *Pueblo* Syndrome," *National Review* 21 (May 20, 1969): 480.

Haggard, M. T. "North Korea's Foreign Policy: "The Meaning of the *Pueblo* and EC-121 Incidents," *Library of Congress Legislative Reference Service* F-384 (June 18, 1969).

Hotz, Robert. "The Flying *Pueblo*," *Aviation Week and Space Technology* 90 (April 28, 1969): 11.

Kim, Joungwon A. "North Korea's New Offensive," *Foreign Affairs* 48:1 (October 1969): 166-179.

"New Lesson in the Limits of Power," *Time* 93 (April 25, 1969): 15-16.

"North Korea Making Trouble Again," *U.S. News and World Report* 66:17 (April 28, 1969): 25-27.

"Remember the EC-121," *National Review* 21 (May 6, 1969): 424.

"Shootdown of a U.S. Navy EC-121 Aircraft," *A Special Historical Study – USAFSS in Korea,* January 1968-April 1969, Extract – Chapter XIII. San Antonio: United States Air Force Security Service (March 15, 1970), pp 105-117. ~~(TSC)~~

Simmons, Robert R.. "The *Pueblo*, EC-121 and Mayaquez Incidents – Some Continuities and Changes," Occasional Papers/Reprints Series in *Contemporary Asian Studies*, #8. Baltimore: University of Maryland School of Law, 1978.

Newspapers

New York Times April-May 1969.

Washington Post April 1969.

Appendix

Crew of the EC-121

GENERAL SERVICE PERSONNEL

OVERSTREET, James H., LCDR, USN (pilot)
GLEASON, David B., LT, USN
SINGER, John H., LT, USN
MC NAMARA, Marshall H., AVMM, USAF

NAVAL SECURITY GROUP PERSONNEL

TAYLOR, Robert F., LT, USN
DUCHARME, Gary R., CT3, USN
LYNCH, Hugh M., SSgt., USMC
MILLER, John A., CT3, USN
POTTS, John H., CT1, USN
RANDALL, Frederick A., CT2, USN
SMITH, Richard E., CTC, USN
SUNDBY, Phillip D., CT3, USN
TESMER, Stephen J., CT2, USN

OTHER MILITARY PERSONNEL

DZEMA, John, LT, USN
PERROTTET, Peter P., LT, USN
RIBAR, Joseph R., LTJG, USN
SYKORA, Robert J., LTJG, USN
WILKERSON, Norman E., LTJG, USN
BALDERMAN, Louis F., AVMM2nd, USAF
CHARTIER, Stephen C., AET1st, USAF
COLGIN, Bernie J., AET1st, USAF
CONNORS, Ballard F., AVMM1st, USAF
HORRIGAN, Dennis J., AET2nd, USAF
GRAHAM, Gene K., AET3rd, USAF
GREINER, LaVerne A., AEMC, USAF
KINCAID, Richard H., AET2nd, USAF
MC NEIL, Timothy H., AET2nd, USAF
PRINDLE, Richard T., Amn, USAF
ROACH, James L., AET1st, USAF
SWEENEY, Richard E., AET1st, USAF
WILLIS, David M., AET3rd, USAF